MUSIC IS LIFE...AND DEATH

MUSIC IS LIFE... AND DEATH

MICHAEL DION

Other Books:
Circle of Chance
The Music Disc Murder
Saratoga Springs

ITI Music Corporation

ITI Music Corporation Publishing

16057 Tampa Palms Bl West

Tampa, FL 33543

ISBN: 978-0-9995684-5-3

Printed and bound in the United States

Cover Graphics: RoxC LLC

www.roxc.graphics/Roxanne Clapp

Cover Photos: Public Domain

Author Photo: Patricia Johnson

To My Wife Laura. Thank you for giving me the time and space to be the creative person I've become in my later years. I also want to commend you for your own endeavors as a serious and yet funny storyteller. Much Love to you as we continue down this path together.

Love to My Daughter, Husband my two grandchildren. I only wish you the best.

And thank you to my family and friends for reading my crazy stories as I become an practicing author, that has a long way to go to be good at it…

I hope you enjoy book number four.

Music is Life…and Death
Chapter 1

Naked and sprawled on the floor, May Ling is stirring from a forced sleep, that saved her life.

The left side of her head hurts like a migraine, as she wakes, beginning to open her eyes, trying to remember what happened, where she was and what she was doing at the time she blacked out.

Ah, she was smashed in her face by a huge man that smelled like garlic. "But Why?", she thinks to herself.

The room comes to life, in this late afternoon, brightened by the colors of red and gold as she gains her sight, mostly from her right eye. She knows that something is wrong with her left eye and reaches up with her hand and touches her face and the area around her left brow.

It's swollen, where the man had hit her. She now recalls with exactness. The pain aches like no other she has ever experienced, but she needs to piece together what occurred.

Straining to look around the room, she remembers that she was with someone in the room when all hell broke loose and that large goon came barging in, kicking the door off its frame.

"Randy," she says quietly, almost to herself. There is no answer. She repeats it twice more, each time louder than before, as she tries to stand up. Still, there is no answer. May Ling then forces herself up on her knees and stands up while looking around the room. She staggers to an ottoman across from where she was standing. She sits down a bit dazed. The room appears to be spinning or "Is it her head" she says to herself?

Gathering up enough strength to stand up again she looks around the two adjoining rooms. They have been trashed, probably done by the goon. Randy and she were making love at the time of their interruption

Replaying in her mind the events she recalls jumping out of bed and running to the door to stop the goon from approaching, only to be cracked in the face and knocked out.

Staggering, walking slowly, May is holding the left side of her face, as she continues to glance around the rooms and yells out this time, "Randy"? Again no one answers. Straining to see, she looks into the bedroom and focuses on where Randy is lying on the floor. As she moves closer to Randy's twisted body, she sees a pool of blood seeping from his head. He is face down. She cautiously kneels next to him and touches the back of his neck. There is no sign of life. He is dead!

In May's short life of 21 years, she never had experienced anything like this before. In Chinatown, there are rules in the brothels. No fighting, no noise, and no death, unless accidental. May knows that this was no accident.

In a trance that is shadowed by the continued throbbing ache in her head and eyes, she is not sure what she should do, or who to call. She is bewildered by the fact that no one heard the scuffle. Why had no one come to their rescue?

Standing up and backing away from Randy's body, May sits down on a nearby chair, completely naked both inwardly and outwardly.

A half hour goes by as she again tries to piece together what had happened and make sense of it. Nothing that she knew or understood could help her figure out why.

Realizing her dilemma, she decided to go to the front office to explain her account of what took place in her room. But first, she had to make herself look presentable.

Sensing that the pain she was feeling on her face was only going to get worse, she went to the icebox, where she found the ice pick hanging from a string. There she chipped some ice away from the block. Then she wrapped it in a nearby towel and placed it on her face.

May then walked into the bathroom and looked into the mirror. Her left cheek was swollen, with a large red bruise that almost covers her eye. Her short black hair seemed to be spiked upwards showing her forehead, where it too was black and blue. Wincing, she washed her face and hands, brushed her hair to restore her bangs and put on her underwear and the Turquoise Blue Mandarin silk dress that she had worn especially for Randy.

After putting on her black slippers, she hurriedly walked downstairs. Normally at the front desk, behind the glassed-in window sat Momma-san or some other bodyguard for the hotel.

"Odd," she thought to herself. There were no sounds inside the building - it was dead quiet. The only noise she heard was the sounds from the traffic outside on Sun Moon Way.

It was June 1942 and now a balmy evening in Los Angeles as May Ling left the Red Dragon Hotel and ran down the street to go back to her apartment. She did not know who to turn to other than to the local Chinatown Tong. After returning to her apartment, she called the neighborhood Chinese "mayor" to set up an appointment to explain to him what had happened to her and Randy.

Music is Life…and Death
Chapter 2

Lounging by the pool, several hours before in the desert, on this dry summer day, Jack Riley was at the home of a well-known Hollywood couple, that she had met at her favorite local restaurant, Pasquale's, only a few nights prior. They had befriended her because of their affection for the military, her stories about her Dad and her own stories of being a private investigator.

Jack looked at her drink that the butler had just handed her. It was so hot that the ice in her glass had almost melted by the time he walked from the inside of the house to where she was sitting. Another guest of the house was a well-known comedian, who was sitting in the shade of the lanai.

Out loud and rather brash he said, "Boy you should see it in August, you can fry an egg on the ground without butter or a pan."

Jack looked at the comic and chuckled to be polite then drank about half of the gin and tonic, licking her lips and stretching out on the chaise lounge.

Almost everyone in tinsel town knew that summer was off-season in Palm Springs. No crowds, no one looking or skulking around taking pictures that would later show up in Life, Look or other magazines. Privacy prevailed, and almost no one would dare go out during the day. But at night the locals frequented one of the many clubs or restaurants, mostly run by the Mob.

The only thing to do in the "Springs" was to eat, tan, drink or prowl the local dives for someone to cuddle up next too. Even though gambling was prevalent in the backrooms, it was never spoken about, unless you didn't want to be seen alive again. At least, that was what she had been told.

Jack had been inactive since her last involvement with the Navy, helping round up some of the espionage crime lords. Taken time off, she had flown to Colorado to see friends before returning home to continue her well needed holiday.

Peering under her large straw hat and oversized sunglasses at the rugged mountain in the distance, Jack was feeling antsy and knew that she needed to start on something new. Though not sure how or what to look for, she thought about calling her Uncle in L.A. to see if he had any outstanding cases that she could work.

Mindlessly placing the gin and tonic to her lips again, she hoped that something would fall into her lap, besides Macy and some of the other retired rich Hollywood elder drunks at the clubs in town. They were always trying to sweet-talk her, even though they were harmless and at the same time "a pain in her ass."

She sure missed Derek, her Navy steady. They had grown very close in such a very short time, but he was sent back to Hawaii after they completed the Mancini case. And now, she didn't quite know when Derek would be calling her, so she tried to entertain herself in any which way she could.

Gazing out towards the mountains, she thought, "Tomorrow, I should go into the office and see if there was anything to investigate, but for the rest of the day, swim, drink, sun, go to dinner and then sleep. It's was just another perfect day."

Music is Life…and Death
Chapter 3

Jimmy Woo was the Mayor for the Chinese Neighborhood, who by reputation, was by far the most honest and understanding of the locals. He had retired to Los Angeles, after serving in the Chinese Navy and became a bit of a hero, having saved an American Navy Captain's life.

In Chinatown, he opened a fresh food market, down the street from the Red Dragon and was the liaison between the Chinese and the City of Los Angeles. He equally had a unique relationship with the Police, since most American major cities had a Chinese population, in which the Tong oversaw. Hence, from the moment the War had started, he had been involved in helping either side out of a jam. This morning would be no different as he was to find out.

As the early morning, California sun was reflecting brightly off the toaster, down the block sat May Ling in her kitchen as she thoughtlessly poured herself another cup of tea. The left side of her face was still swollen, even after icing it down for a long time last night.

Inattentively she stirred the cup looking deep into the color of the green tea. She was trying to remember every detail that had occurred the previous night. Randy had acted strangely coming through the back of the building to her apartment before they left for the Red Dragon. He had given May a manila envelope to hold onto and said, "I will pick this up in the morning." He then made her hide it in a safe place and made sure that she would remember where she kept it. He acted so peculiar that he had a hard time calming down, even during their lovemaking. And when he did fall asleep, he was mumbling and very restless. May recollected that it took her a long time to fall asleep as well, as there seemed to be something in the air that kept her hovering.

May couldn't help but think that Randy's murder might be connected to a local Chinese member. But after running down the stairs of the hotel and finding no one at the front desk, she didn't understand, since the brothel belonged to Mr. Chung, who was precise and strict about the rules for the hotel. All she knew was that Randy was dead and didn't know why.

May stood up after finishing her tea and looked at the clock. It was nearly 8:15 as she grabbed her purse and keys and headed towards the door to go over to the Mayor's location. She stopped and turned around and went to the spot in the wall where she had hidden the envelope, given to her by Randy. She peeled the wallpaper back and took it out and neatly placed it in her purse. She then pushed the wallpaper back against the wall and moved a small table close to it. She wanted to make sure that nothing looked abnormal or out of place.

As she started to walk towards the door again, she heard heavy footsteps coming up the stairs and her landlady yelling from the first floor, "White men not allowed in this building!"

A rush of adrenalin filled May as she panicked and almost leaped to the window, opening it just as she heard the doorknob turning. Wasting no time, she hopped through the window unto the fire escape and headed down to the ground.

Fortunately, she was only one flight up and just as she reached the bottom, she turned her head towards her window and saw the Italian thug, who had smashed her face in the brothel and was looking straight at her. He cussed at her as she ran down the alley, then out onto the street towards the area close to the Red Dragon.

Jimmy Woo was sweeping off the morning dust from his sidewalk when May Ling ran up to him out of breath.

Jimmy said, "May, why are you running?"

May turned in the direction of where her apartment was and pointed.

Jimmy looked down the street towards the apartment to see two men getting into a car and gently ushered May through the door into the store, as he continued to sweep. He told her, "Go, go inside and hide!"

The black four-door Ford, drove by very slowly as the two men looked both right and left, trying to see where May had gone. Jimmy moved his body around to watch them as they looked directly at him, driving past his store.

Jimmy remembered seeing one of them when the Italians had come to Chinatown and burnt down Mr. Chung's restaurant. However, the driver looked like Asian descent and he'd not seen him before, but the shotgun rider was the driver for Carmen Ialucci, he was sure of it.

The car moved slowly down the street without incident and then turned the corner at the next light. Jimmy spoke to May from the street, "Bié ràng rén kàn jiàn" (stay out of sight), as he continued to sweep the sidewalk. After ten minutes, Jimmy went back inside to find May crouched down in a corner.

Jimmy looked at her and said, "Stand up, let's go upstairs, and you can tell me all about it."

Calling his wife to come down and mind the store, Jimmy escorted May upstairs into the kitchen area, where there was only one window, but was out of sight of anyone looking up at it.

Sitting down Jimmy asked May to tell him what happened. She did. Then May opened her purse and handed the envelope to Jimmy. He didn't open it. He wanted to make sure that he could resolve the immediate concerns of May and keep her protected.

Jimmy knew that whenever the Italians came into Chinatown, there was always trouble. He reckoned that whatever was inside the envelope was enough to get somebody killed, as in the case of Randy, so he decided to arrange the local Chinese Tong protection for May.

Jimmy told May that he would contact Mr. Chung and that he would know what to do. In the meantime, she was to remain with him and his wife. He asked her if she needed anything from her apartment and she nodded. So they made a list and then called her landlady.

Mrs. Cho was very upset and was ranting to Jimmy that the Italians had made a mess in May's apartment looking for something and she and the rest of the apartment dwellers were cleaning up her torn-up apartment. Jimmy asked Mrs. Cho to have Laura Lee, who was her next-door neighbor to gather up some personal items and bring them to his store, no questions asked.

Mrs. Cho started to say something when Jimmy interrupted, "Mrs. Cho, we will make sure that you are safe, and we will make sure that we pay for any extra expenses that you have incurred from this incident."

Calming herself down, Mrs. Cho thanked Jimmy and hung up the phone.

Jimmy then called Mr. Chung and spoke in Mandarin about what had happened and that there was a dead body in the Red Dragon Hotel.

Mr. Chung told Jimmy that he would send his men over to clean it up and to report back to him with their findings.

He then advised Jimmy, "Keep May with you and your wife and come by tomorrow at 3 PM. By then I will have some additional information about this break in the truce between our Italian Brothers and Chinatown."

Jimmy hung up the phone and told May to follow him to a bedroom that was not in use. He gave her a Chinese herb sedative and told her to rest. In the meantime, he would be downstairs in his store.

May did as she was told and quickly found herself in a deep sleep, fighting off the horrible pictures of the Italian goon and Randy's dead body.

Music is Life…and Death
Chapter 4

Jack woke up early on Thursday and busily fixed her breakfast of two eggs over medium, a slice of ham, and toast with marmalade. She felt nervous during this morning, even without the first cup of coffee. She detected that something had occurred and that the gods of destiny were sending out a message to her. She just couldn't read or receive it yet in her mind.

"Those gods," she thought, "are sometimes sweet and bring roses and candy, yet they also can be angry and bitter and bring vinegar and compost for you to make something out of it. What would it be this time?"

Unlike her "War Time Sisters" riveting in bib overalls or working in offices wearing dresses, Jack outfitted herself in a lightweight linen navy blue pinstripe pantsuit with a darker navy-blue blouse. Because of the imposed shortages in many materials during the war, women's dresses were mostly floral prints or geometric patterns, and of course, there were no stockings. Nylon had a higher calling since it was used to replace silk for parachutes. Some women would draw black lines on the back of their legs to look like stockings. Trousers increased its popularity particularly for young and working women and were usually khaki or dark green while wedges replaced high heels.

Hanging on one of the other chairs in the kitchen was her coat. It was white with a white handkerchief rising from within the pocket pointing upwards like a mountain peak.

Sitting down, looking deep into the plate, she absentmindedly buttered her toast and then put a dollop of jam on each side. She looked through the toast into space, zoning out of where she was at that moment.

Just as she was about to take her first bite of toast, the telephone rang. It immediately jarred her back to reality. She placed the toast down and got up to walk over to the phone in the living room. For just a moment, time stood still. Jack felt strange as if she was about to receive another "call of death," like the time the phone rang at her house this early in the morning and a Navy Medical Officer told her that her Dad had passed away.

She looked down at the phone, hesitated for a moment and then quickly regained her confidence and picked up the ringing device.

"Hello," Jack spoke assertively.

"Jacqueline, is that you? This is Jimmy Woo in Los Angeles. I am sorry if I have awakened you, but I would like to ask for your help. It could be a matter of Life and Death!"

Jack stepped back from where she was standing, with the phone still pressed up against her ear. It was as if she already knew that this would be the call to ramp her up, bring the excitement of a case. Her adrenaline began to pump harder and faster. Her breasts began to heave, but she paused before she answered, knowing that she was smiling inside and out. The anxiety of taking on another case was subsiding. She was whole again, and ready to engage in whatever Jimmy needed.

"Jimmy" she finally said. "Yes, I am here for you. What can I do?"

Jimmy explained May Ling's story. When he finished, Jack agreed to meet with him at Mr. Chung's. Meanwhile, Jack would check in with her Uncle Mike to see if he knew of anything.

As the call ended, Jack placed the phone back into its cradle. Her initial intuition was that it pointed towards the Mob. Who else would have killed a music transcriber and why would anyone trash an apartment? Perhaps they weren't looking for something that belonged to them or wanted to control. And why would they go after May? If she didn't know better, this had signs of one of the L.A. Mafia families.

Reaching out for her Uncle at the precinct she found that he was not available, so Jack called Melvin, her mechanic at PS Melvin's Garage on Indian Canyon Rd.

"Big Red" was being tended to for her summer service. Palm Springs is so bloody hot that if you don't keep the radiator filled with coolant, you might as well leave your car in the desert. Since the War, properties of anti-freeze were now used to support coolant for summer driving. It was better than just water since it lasted much longer.

Melvin was up to his normal jokester status. "Jack, your car is ready. Don't tell me you are heading to L.A. to get it smashed up again?"

No mood for his snide remarks, Jack just listened and told Melvin she'd be by in an hour or so after she went to her office to pick up a few things.

After locking up her house, she stepped into the loaner from Melvin and headed to her office. At 9 AM, it was already 89 degrees. Today would be a scorcher in the desert, but fortunately, L.A. would be a whole lot cooler, maybe 80 or so and livable.

Jack's office was on the main street, in a two-story building on Palm Canyon Dr, which was the entrance or exit of the town. The only thing closest to her office was the park leading to the San Jacinto Mountain.

The building was like most of the Spanish façade buildings in downtown Palm Springs with tiled floors, tiled roofs and stucco sides, and no elevator.

Walking through the main entrance into the lobby, you were greeted by a receptionist who acted as your employee, even if all the other tenants shared the services provided by the building's owner.

On this specific morning, Libby was extremely chatty as Jack walked straight up to her desk.

Libby said, "Good Morning Jack, you have had visitors already. As a matter of fact, they were here when I got here, waiting for you. Of course, I sent them away, but promised I would give you their information and folder. They were a bit brash, but you know me, nothing surprises me these days, so I told them to get lost, else I'd call the cops on them."

Jack thanked Libby for her assistance and told her that she would make sure that those guys paid her the proper respect the next time.

Taking the sealed envelope from her, Jack proceeded to climb the stairs to her office.

Unlocking the door, she was greeted by a foreign smell, in a stuffy room that had not been used for a while. The odor was from some sort of cheap cologne that hung in the air, like the smoke from an all-night poker game.

Aware that they had been in her office already looking for something she thought to herself,

"What could it be that I might have for whoever was looking through the drawers and file cabinets?"

Nothing seemed to be out of place, but Jack could feel that someone had looked at everything and once again commented to herself, "It's always an unpleasant feeling to know that if someone other than yourself has been touching your belongings. It's like you have been touched by dirty hands and want to take a bath to rid yourself of that smell and feel of such displeasure."

Deciding to keep her door opened, she turned on the two fans that sat on knee-high tables. Then she opened the blinds to let the hot sun penetrate the room to rid herself of the odor hopefully.

Sitting on her desk chair, she opened the envelope. No address was on the outside, but inside there was a contract that was unsigned by a famous L.A. songwriter, Donnie Heaven but signed by Joey Barcelino, a reputed mob boss.

Jack raised her eyebrow as she continued to read. She knew about Barcelino who seemed to have his fingers knee deep into the entertainment business. He worked with the Chicago guys in the up and coming Las Vegas syndicate, by controlling many of the incoming and outgoing film stars and music business artists.

Brushing the hair aside from her face, Jack continued to look over the document. It was a contract controlling all the songs ever written from this singer, lyricist, and songwriter. It also had an end date that read "infinite!"

Along with the contract was a three-page letter from a new record company, Velvet Tone Records that included Donnie's signature.

Donnie had acquired the rights to the defunct name from Columbia Records since it had been out of business since 1932.

For its continued use of the name, Donnie made a deal with Columbia where they would receive one penny for each unit sold forever.

The contract had signatures from two other famous, notable performers from the entertainment world. All three would share one-third of the profits that the record company would receive, from all sales and publishing.

Attached to the contract was a rider page that listed several well-known names from the music side of the business. It included singers, band leaders and other soloists that had already signed on to release their records.

It all looked legit but as Jack would later find out, "Donnie didn't want to be part of this record company because the percentage to the Mob would be 50%. And though Donnie wanted to establish his own record company in L.A., he wanted it to be outside the control of the Syndicate."

As Jack remembered reading about it, some reporters stated that The Chicago Mobsters had already infiltrated the musician's union by befriending Jimmy Petrillo, who now controlled the American Federation and the "who, what, when and where" the musicians would play for and record. Remembering an article that Jack recently read in Variety, there was rumbling that Petrillo was going to instill a ban to shut out the musicians from recording, but because of the War, no one thought that he would do such a thing.

Unlike the early silent years of the movies, when the musicians "played live" in the theaters, now the only place they played was in the movies themselves. So, Petrillo tried to hold up the movie studios until he got what he wanted.

It was blackmail at its finest. Because of such control, Petrillo did not permit the record labels from distributing their records when a ban was in place. However, unlike some of the other record labels, Capitol Records was owned by songwriter and singer Johnny Mercer. Through the company, he was able to promote its recordings at the radio stations and sales dramatically increased which caused Petrillo and the Mob much aggravation.

Meanwhile, the Chicago Mob muscled their way into the clubs, jukeboxes, record stores, and record companies. They tried to hold them all "hostage" unless they paid for (to the Mob) the privilege of recording, selling and playing their music.

Jack pondered what all this meant. She knew of both men in these documents, but she didn't quite see the connection other than Donnie's name printed on both documents. Was he thumbing his nose at Joey and going out on his own? Did Joey own Donnie and whatever he wrote? What was the connection and why was she sent this information?

Jack leaned back in her chair and was in deep thought when the phone rang. It was Libby. She said she had a call from a Mr. Barcelino and asked if Jack would take it.
She said, "Yes, Libby, Thank you."

Libby patched Barcelino through and after Jack said, "Hello," the first thing she heard through the phone was a loud wheeze, right before any words came out of his mouth.

"Miss Riley," a deep and dark voice came through the phone.

"Yes," Jack replied.

"My name is Mr. Joey Barcelino. Just "Joey" to my friends. Have you heard of me?"

Again, Jack said, "Yes."

"Good, then I don't have to waste my time enlightening you about how powerful I am and what I represent and what I do to people who betray my trust!"

"Christ," Jack thought, "Who does this guy think he is and then she remembered... He is extremely dangerous, so I had better be careful how I answer his questions."

"Miss Riley, you have received an envelope that my associates have dropped off, Yes?"

"Yes," Jack responded as calmly as she could.

"You have read the contract and letter then?"

"Yes," Jack said, but now she was getting tired of answering in one syllable words.

"Then you must know why I called?"

This time, it was Jack's turn and said, "Actually, I haven't the foggiest idea why you sent me these and NO, I do not know why you are calling me!"

Upset by Barcelino's rudeness, Jack continued, "And furthermore, how in the hell did you get my number? I am minding my own business in the desert, and you have people dropping off documents at my office that I am supposed to know why? I am afraid not. So again, unless you can justify this conversation, then I would say we are through!"

Barcelino, sensing Jack's temper started to wheeze again and then replied. "Perhaps we are getting off on the wrong foot, Miss Riley. I merely wanted to give you some background before I ask you for some assistance in finding a lost article of mine. You see, I am a very busy person, and my associates are also. Or should I say too busy to find such things, so I was hoping that you could tear yourself away from the heat of Palm Springs and come to L.A. to find these documents that are by the very nature of the contract you are holding, MINE! And for the record, the Ialucci Family sent your name to me in case I needed some help!"

Jack now knew she needed to be extra cautious with her response since he was referred by a sworn enemy.

Backing down slightly, Jack said, "Mr. Barcelino, I would like to help you but a new case just became my major concern, and I don't think that I could help you or find your documents until I finish with my prior commitment. I do appreciate it very much that you called me. But I do not think that I can be of service to you now and would be extremely happy if I could recommend someone else locally in the L.A. area that probably could do the same for you as I could. May I give you their name?"

Barcelino knew that he was getting nowhere with Jack. She didn't bite on his request. Without mentioning it, he begged off for now until he could be sure that she wasn't involved with May Ling or the Chinese. So, he politely said, "Thank you" and hung up.

Jack seethed as she set the phone back down. Why was this "Italian Jerk" really calling her, she said to herself. "The Bloody Italians; what were they into now?"

When Jack got the chance to speak to her Uncle Mike, she would let him know about Barcelino and the contract that she was holding.

Leaning back in her chair, she took out her handkerchief and blotted her forehead. She had perspired a bit talking to Barcelino, so much so that her underarms were so wet that stains were now on her blouse. She cursed Barcelino. She knew that he was no good.

Stripping off the stained blouse, she looked through one of the mahogany drawers, for another off-white shirt to wear.

As she was finishing with the buttons she thought; "Now I have to worry if someone is tailing me again. And what about this contract that was now face down on her desk?"

A puzzle for sure thought Jack. She had to get on the road to L.A. to see Mr. Chung. Time was of the essence now.

Music is Life…and Death
Chapter 5

In Hollywood at the Brown Derby, Donnie Heaven sat at
the bar. He lit his Lucky Strike with his zippo engraved
lighter that read, "Someday," which was given to him by
his friend, Dicky Linsky for his first hit song.

But here Donnie was at only 12:30 in the afternoon
ordering a gin martini. He had to have a drink to calm
down. Just an hour before, he had a visitor, none other than
the muscle man, Mickey Bucco, courtesy of Barcelino.
Across the street, Mickey had barged into his office, and
threatened Donnie that if he didn't sign the solid clad
agreement with Barcelino for life, along with his two
partners that all hell would break loose!

This agreement was to establish Velvet Tone Records to
compete with Johnny Mercer, who had done the same thing
independently without the Mob. The only problem was
that his fourth partner in Donnie's company would be Joey
Barcelino.

Donnie knew that the other partners would probably never
go for the idea, so what could he do to stay alive and own
the record company of his dreams, and at the same time
keep Barcelino from taking half if not more of all the
profits while he continued to control Donnie for life.

Donnie pondered his dilemma as he took the first sip from
the ice-cold drink. The bartender Marcos at the Derby
knew how to make them just right, not too dry and not too
wet.

Donnie's thoughts drifted back to a time in Chicago when
life began as carefree and exciting when he was starting in

the music business. Though he was a poor immigrant kid from the East Side, he would travel the clubs and the restaurants uptown, singing and playing his music for anyone who would listen. Unfortunately, or fortunately, his number one fan and main listener, became his benefactor who was a young up and comer mobster by the name of Joey Barcelino.

Joey had taken a shine to the young man and began to support Donnie by setting him up in an apartment, making sure he had appropriate clothes for his gigs and eventually finding him lovers (male and female). To this end, Joey had become Donnie's pimp, finding not only jobs but other singers that would perform his songs, which were promoted at radio or in movies that the Mob controlled. Like some other well-known singers and actors, Donnie had become a celebrity at the expense of the Mob. And with each year, Barcelino became more important to Chicago, and higher up within the hierarchy in the Outfit and so Donnie never had to worry about money or anything else.

Fatefully, as a heavy gambler, Donnie lost everything that he had earned. Realizing this, Joey wanted to retain Donnie permanently.

Joey needed to be repaid for his time and efforts, so one day he handed Donnie a contract that would guarantee a 50% cut of everything that Donnie had written and everything Donnie would write in the future. There was no ending date entered in the contract.

Even back in those days, neither men knew that they would end up in Los Angeles, and in a way controlling each other's destiny.

While the Mob had looked the other way during the beginning of Donnie's career, they now looked at Donnie in the same way that Joey saw him, a money maker and that was something that they wanted to control.

As Donnie pondered his situation, sitting in the restaurant, to his left a few stools away, sat a platinum blonde in an almost see-through white blouse, tan linen skirt, and white shoes.

Donnie looked her up and down and noticed that her shoes matched her blouse. "Is that Marilyn?" he thought? "No, it couldn't be, but then… oh well, right now I need to concentrate on my own life."

Finishing his drink, Donnie waived at the bartender, paid his bill, then lit another cigarette as he left to go back to his office. He decided he would call his partners "Bebop" Buster and Alan Glass and explain the situation to them.

Bebop owned one of the local record shops, and Alan was a Hollywood attorney that Donnie began to use as he made money writing songs and performing.

Tinsel Town and New York now controlled most of the music and entertainment businesses. So that is where the writers and composers all lived and worked. (ASA was one of the largest agencies that controlled many stars, writers, producers, and musicians).

On the West Coast, the LA Studios were everywhere throughout the City and the musicals being cranked out only lent itself to more songwriters and record companies trying to find the next hit.

Bebop's prominent record store was called "The Hollywood Hot Licks." Inside against a window and side wall sat a grand piano. There on a small sound stage was a sound booth that was used to showcase both unknown talent and known singers and sometimes, dancers.

All the great singers would come by his joint when they were in town. It kept everyone close, like a family. The singers never got out of touch with their fans, especially during the War. It was a place that added romance to the girls working at the plants all day long, waiting for their husbands or boyfriends.

Sometimes the crowd overflowed unto the street in front of the store after working all day so that they could see who would turn up and sing. It was always a busy locale, and many hearts were made and broken at "The Licks."

Down the highway, in San Diego, "Mob" member Frank Bompensiero also owned a record store, amongst other local money-making operations. He was forever pressuring Bebop to sell him the famed "Hot Licks" store, but Bebop continued to refuse the offer. And though the Mob threatened Bebop from time to time, they never laid a hand on him.

Perhaps it was because the store paid big money to the record labels, that were controlled by the Mob for selling all those records.

Likewise, through underground casinos that the Mob controlled, they operated and controlled the jukebox operations throughout most of the major cities and had tremendous influence in the movie industry.

Truth be told, while the government pretended to shut down, lock up some of the major criminals, they looked the other way, so businesses carried on here and there at the corner drugstore or club.

At these places of entertainment that Chicago owned or controlled, they were a "one-stop" shop that laundered money, controlled live music, studios, manufacturing and the distribution of records.

Bebop was Donnie's first call.

Bebop's response was to go ahead and "make the deal" with Joey but counter an offer that after two years he would only receive 10%, not the 50% that he wanted to take. He then told Donnie to get Joey to agree to give up all future rights to new songs that Donnie would write.

Bebop being like an Uncle said, "Besides Kid, what do you have to lose. You might never again write a hit song!"

Donnie laughed and told Bebop that he'd try, but first, he'd talk this over with Alan, to make sure that from the legal side Donnie would never again be in the hole with Barcelino.

Unfortunately for Donnie, the partying and gambling is what caused him to get in the hole in the first place. He had hocked everything he owned and then made a deal with Joey to be able to live like he was a big-time writer and star. No one knew that Donnie was broke and that it was only through Joey's "good heart" that Donnie could act like a celebrity!

By the time Donnie had gotten done with all his work for the day, including approving a musical composition for one of the dancer's songs in the newest Solomon's Brothers musical, it was late afternoon, and Donnie couldn't get a hold of Alan before he left his office.

Alan's phone kept ringing which was kind of strange since he had a secretary, who normally was there till almost 9 PM every night.

One of Donnie's calls made that day was to schedule an appointment with one of the Hollywood actresses and her husband, who had just gotten back from New York. Donnie wanted her to sing a few songs in a new movie that he was signed on to complete the music score. Though not a singer by trade, the actress expanded herself to the role very nicely and her voice would match the sequence of melodies that pieced together the storyline.

They were to meet at The Bombay Room which was located nearly on the corner of La Brea and Santa Monica. It wasn't far from Hollywood Blvd. and was one of the "darling spots" for the in-crowd of movie stars and entertainment industry moguls. It was a Chinese restaurant with a flair for Americana thrown into each dish. The main room was lit up like a Christmas tree, and the place was generally noisy from all the laughter and "loudmouth" entertainers always showing off.

When Donnie arrived at the restaurant, Alice Ray (sometimes mistaken for Alice Faye) and Dick Linsky were having their second round of drinks with a host of friends who all gathered by the piano in the center of the room. Lots of smiles and giggles came from their direction as Donnie casually walked over to where they were standing.

Outside, shortly after the early happy hour, Mickey Bucco drove his Buick to the valet stand in front of the restaurant and nodded to the passenger. The Asian slipped out of the car door, looked at the attendant, who backed away when he saw the Asian carrying a sub-machine gun. The Asian then sauntered to the open doors of The Bombay.

As Donnie stood next to Dick, smiles became fearful glances and frightened stares as glass shattered and almost everyone in the restaurant dropped to the floor in horror. Donnie was amongst them, having done so, reacting to the sounds of gunfire.

In the doorway, Kim Koto had stopped, stood still for a moment, hesitated, then smiled and began emptying his weapon on the inside dinners. When the cartridge clip was empty, he turned and walked swiftly back to the waiting car that sped off into the orange horizon dusk.

As quickly as the thundering noise reverberated throughout the restaurant from the gunfire, so too did the deadly silence that overwhelmed the room. Then paused screams blurted out as the crowd became alive, knowing what had just happened. Some of the patrons started yelling and scrambling, grabbing their things and running out the doors.

Donnie stood up and looked around the room, not sure what he was looking for, but when he turned back around, he looked for Alice and Dick, and as his eyes moved downward, he found Dick's eyes wide open and dead!

Alice was clutching him and crying so loud that it penetrated the screams of the other patrons in the restaurant.

Donnie stooped down and got on one knee as he looked at Dick's face and then at Alice. What could he say? Donnie quickly placed his hand over Dick's face and closed his dead eyes. He then took hold of Alice and slowly stood up. Donnie looked straight into Alice's eyes. She was in shock and speechless now, and all he could do was to place his arms around her and hold her as she continued to sob.

It was less than five minutes before the sound of the police cars could be heard. Fire engine trucks roared behind them as part of the standard city policy in case there was a fire.

The first policeman to run into the restaurant was Sergeant McCarthy, with his gun drawn. One of the city's finest Irish cops, he was also a talented tenor singer that had appeared on several of Donnie's recordings.

McCarthy was from the La Brea Station which was also the precinct location of one of Donnie's oldest friends, Captain Michael O'Keefe. The Captain came pushing through the doorway right behind McCarthy yelling and waving his left arm, with his revolver held close to his side in his right hand.

They both stopped and looked around to see that some of the patrons in the restaurant where Donnie and Alice who were now crouched back on the floor.

No one moved for a moment until the two cops began to speak. Then almost simultaneously everyone stood up and began to talk at the same time.

In his broken English, Captain O'Keefe told everyone to "Please shut up and stop moving!"

The Captain then looked over in the direction of Donnie and Alice and walked closer to where they were. Several pairs of police officers entered through the front and rear doors. They then began to take each patron and restaurant worker outside for questioning.

"O'Keefe, over here," Donnie whispered out loud, as he stopped in front of him.

"Donnie are you two alright?", he responded.

Standing up almost alone in the center of the room Donnie said, "Kind of," but then turned to his side so Captain O'Keefe could see Alice sitting on the floor, cradling Dick in her lap.

Looking at Alice, O'Keefe stooped down and took her hand. She stood up, almost floating, making no sound at all, as O'Keefe guided her to the doors leading to the street. By this time, newspaper photographers and reporters were all outside snapping shots and tugging at the arms and lives of the poor souls who only wanted a good meal, but instead found themselves in the middle of a murder.

O'Keefe escorted Alice over to McCarthy, who was now at the door and told him, "Please take Ms. Ray home. I want twenty-four-hour surveillance at her house. Make sure you contact the studio she is under contract with, so they can send over some help. And get someone over to Dick Linsky's house and find out what you can. I'll either be here or at the station."

O'Keefe closed the doors of the restaurant on the photographers who kept popping pictures of Donnie standing there alone in the middle of the restaurant. Unconcerned and unrelenting reporters didn't care that "Death in Hollywood" was on the menu today.

Music is Life…and Death
Chapter 6

Jack had gotten to the Palm Springs Garage at 1:15 PM. It was a scorcher in the Springs at 101 degrees in the shade. Melvin was smiling at Jack, telling her to be extra careful with Big Red, as she waved to him and made a right turn out of the garage and started her way to LA.

Before leaving she called her Aunt Dorothy and asked if she could spend the night. Her Aunt was quite pleased to hear from her and told Jack that her room would be ready. She then tried calling her Uncle at the precinct but was told that he was investigating a shooting.

As she drove along Route 111 with the rugged mountain of San Jacinto along one side of the road, Jack pondered Donnie's contract and the call from Barcelino. She had wished that she could have gotten a hold of her Uncle, but soon enough she would be there to inquire what he knew about this thug.

As Jack reached Riverside, she thought she caught a glimpse of a large black Cadillac staying about four car lengths behind her. She made a mental note but thought that maybe she was overreacting because of her prior case, or the phone calls from Barcelino and Jimmy.

It was almost 3:45 when she pulled into a Texaco station. As she got out of the car to visit the restroom, she noticed that the Caddie had pulled into the station behind the Buick. "Caution" set her wits in motion, but she went inside to the women's room just the same. After finishing her business and stepping outside, she observed that the Caddie was no longer by the gasoline pumps.

Jack then paid the attendant and got back into her convertible and drove to the end of the station.

Looking left to make sure it was clear she pulled into the highway and continued her drive to L.A.

About four miles up the road, as she looked into her rear view mirror, she saw the Caddie. The hairs on the back of her neck seemed to stand straight up. She now knew that the call from Joey Barcelino and whatever the contract was about, was pulling her into something that would require her to be extra careful. Did Jimmy's phone call connect to Barcelino? Perhaps time would tell once she got to the City!

When Jack arrived in L.A., it was almost 5 PM.

Carefully she drove the long way to Chinatown, to see if she could make out whoever was in the Caddie. Driving through the streets, the Caddie had inched its way up and was now right behind her Buick. It followed her as she drove down the block to where Mr. Chung's restaurant was situated.

Pulling into the entrance of the restaurant the Caddie sped forward and past the Dragon House Restaurant. Perfectly, she could make out both the driver and the passenger in the front seat. She remembered seeing their pictures in an article that she was just finished reading the other day, lounging by the pool. The caption indicated them as "business associates" of the infamous Joey Barcelino.

Jack didn't mind if she was used for something good, but the fact that this crime boss already had people shadowing her, expressed that she was already into something dangerous.

As Jack got out of the car, she grabbed her purse and took out the memo book, jotted down the license number along with the type of car. She would give this information to her Uncle to check on who the car was registered too.

Once she reached the steps of the restaurant, the huge carved out dragon shape rosewood double doors opened, and two well-armed Chinese bodyguards appeared with very little expression on their faces. They just bowed as Jack walked through the doorway.

She was curious about how they could have known that someone was entering the restaurant. Then she noticed the hidden cameras on both walls inside the door.

She would have to commend Mr. Chung for the protection of his premises.

Once inside Jack was greeted by a Chinese girl, with short black hair, in a black and green silk mandarin dress. Her slippers were black with green dragons embroidered on the tops, and she wore green eye shadow to match the color of the dress. All she said was, "Please follow me!"

Walking the length of the restaurant, Jack followed the Chinese girl to a hallway that ran alongside the restaurant and then in a circular path to stairs that led to the next floor. When they arrived at the top of the stairs, two more bodyguards were about to stop Jack and the girl from entering, when they heard Mr. Chung's voice.

"Let Jack and Lily Song enter."

With that, the two guards moved back into position along the wall and were almost invisible against the darkened hallway.

Puzzled, Jack could almost imagine how much secret gadgets the old Chinese man had inside his building, then said, "Greetings Mr. Chung" in her most pleasant voice.

Mr. Chung replied, "And to you Jack, my most favorite private investigator. How have you been?"

"I've been good Mr. Chung, but then if I weren't here, I wouldn't be able to help you out again."

Mr. Chung chuckled as Jack heard Jimmy's voice saying hello from the stairs.

Jimmy walked up to Jack and put his arms around her and gave her a warm hug.

He said, "Jack, I am sorry to call you up and ask for your help in this matter, but since it's a Chinese girl and an American boy, I thought that I should call you first before we contact your Uncle."

Jack said to Jimmy, "You were right to call me first; besides it was time for me to leave the calmness of the desert and get back into the trials and tribulations of real-life in the city."

Jimmy smiled and then Mr. Chung requested, "Please sit down."

Moments later, the girl who had brought Jack upstairs, was back in the room with a tray of tea and some finger sandwiches.

Jack looked at Mr. Chung with some surprise. He said, "Too many travels to London. I like those cucumber sandwiches the best!"

After Lily Song poured the tea, she left the room and Jimmy began his story about May Ling.

Mr. Chung nodded his head occasionally but said nothing until Jimmy was finished.

Jimmy then handed Jack the large envelope and asked her to look at the contents. As Jack opened it, she noticed one common name that she had just seen on another document, Donnie Heaven. It was sheets of music and a contract with only Donnie's name on it. The title of the song was, "Finally I'm Free," and there was a note attached to the music that said, "Alice Ray to sing in the new movie of the same title."

Jack looked at Jimmy and then at Mr. Chung. It was Mr. Chung who spoke first.

"Jack, I now have May Ling in protective care. I know of this Donnie Heaven, and I have asked my contacts to keep me informed of who he does business with and his whereabouts. I know that he is fairly famous, but I have also found out that he is connected and in business with a certain Mr. Joey Barcelino."

Chung continued, "Mr. Barcelino is no particular friend of the Chinese people. He has a long arm that stretches across these United States and has infiltrated many established law enforcement agencies, city governments, as well as the U.S. Military. Apparently, he has several so-called honest contracts in the entertainment business that supposedly keeps the government from sending him back to Italy. That said, he has from time to time upset some of the Chinese towns that I and my other brethren monitor, so it is in our best interest to make sure that he is kept under control and out of our Chinese businesses and neighborhoods."

Jack knew what Chung was saying. But in her mind, she suspected that Barcelino was now a major player, who seemed to take the place of the Mancini family after their round up just a month ago.

Jack was mentally putting pieces of the puzzle together in her head when Jimmy broke the silence.

"Jack, does this mean anything to you? Something is puzzling about who was looking for May Ling. It seems that the Italians also have an Asian working with them, but so far we have not been able to find out who he is!"

"Jimmy," Jack said, "Yes, it just so happens' that Barcelino called me this morning and started talking to me about a contract that he had signed with Donnie and that he had lost something mighty important to him. It appears this is what he was talking to me about. I can't be 100% sure but I think it could be. I will need to do some more poking around to see what I can find out.

Hopefully, my Uncle can shed some light on this tonight when I see him. Now, what about this Asian fellow? Does anyone know anything, who he is or why he's working with them?"

Mr. Chung chimed in that he would "look into it" since the Italians had broken the truce by coming into Chinatown and killing an American. He then asked if he could be of any other assistance.

Jack asked Mr. Chung to keep Randy's documents in a safe place and that she would contact him if she needed them or assistance.

As she was leaving, Jack promised to stay in touch, then they all bowed to each other.

Walking outside to her car, she looked at her watch and saw that it was nearly 7 PM. Feeling a bit hungry as she began the drive to the Valley to spend the night with her Uncle and Aunt, she hoped that Aunt Dorothy had something left over for her to eat.

As Jack turned onto La Brea toward Hollywood, she kept her eyes opened for any tagalongs. When she reached Sunset Blvd., she made a right. There in the corner of her rearview mirror, she saw the Caddie again. She thought to herself that she probably should have taken up the offer from Mr. Chung, but then again, she was going to her Uncle's house and perhaps Barcelino's thugs would leave well enough alone there.

Over Cahuenga Blvd, Jack drove Big Red and came to a traffic light at Ventura Blvd. The Caddie was behind her as she drove a few more streets and then turned right onto Hortense where her Uncle and Aunt lived. The Caddie drove in the same direction as if it was going to follow her, but then stopped and made a U-turn and headed back towards Hollywood. It seemed to know who lived on the street.

When Jack rang the door, it was 7:45.

Aunt Dorothy opened the door with a great big smile on her face. "Welcome Home, Jacqueline."

Jack smiled and kissed her Aunt on the cheek and hugged her.

"Come in," Aunt Dorothy said, as she closed the door behind Jack. Just then Uncle Mike came into the foyer from the living room where Jack was standing.

"Well just don't stand there me lass, come give your Uncle a big kiss!"

Jack smiled and walked over to her Uncle and planted her lips on both sides of his cheeks, leaving behind her lip impressions in red. He smiled and then gently wiped them away.

Jack beamed and said, "Glad to see you both and boy am I famished! What's for dinner?"

"Sit down" Aunt Dorothy replied. "I'll get you a plate. We have already eaten, as we know you sometimes run a tad bit late", smiling as she went into the kitchen.

Jack laughed. "Oh yeah, like I know what time is normal!" Then they all giggled, and Jack ate while her Uncle and Aunt asked lots of questions and of course Jack answered them in between the bites of Irish meatloaf (made with beef and pork and Guinness Stout) and a half glass of the same beer to wash it down.

After dinner, Aunt Dorothy and Jack chatted like girls do, while making up her bed for the overnight stay.

Meanwhile, Uncle Mike was in the living room listening to the news on the radio. There was the usual news about the war. It seemed that that was the bulk of what everyone heard these days. Where the "Boys" were and how they were doing. Sometimes it was good, and other times it seemed like America was losing hundreds of sailors and soldiers.

When Jack joined her Uncle in the living room, Benny Goodman was playing the song "Stardust" and singing it was Donnie Heaven. It was a good intro for Jack to tell her Uncle her story of the past twenty-four hours, though leaving out the part of the documents and the kid found dead in Chinatown, at least for the moment. (Randy's body was turned over to the LAPD several days after his murder courtesy of Mr. Chung).

When Jack had finished, her Uncle looked at her and said, "Jesus Jack, Barcelino! You have got to get out from under that situation, whatever it is. The guy is by far one of the most dangerous criminals we have in the city at the moment and maybe in the States. He'd just as soon as look at you as kill you. You are not safe!"

Looking away and then back at Jack, her Uncle continued, "Just this afternoon I was at a crime scene with Donnie, where a famous friend of his was killed, in broad daylight at a restaurant. The L.A. Chief is on everyone's back to get the city in order and find out who in the hell did this."

Surprised, Jack asked, "Who was at the restaurant with Donnie?"

"Alice Ray and Dick Linsky," answered her Uncle. "And poor Dick is the one who got shot! Jesus, I can't imagine who'd want Dick killed? He had no known enemies."

"Perhaps it wasn't Dick they were aiming for," Jack replied.

Her Uncle was looking down at his shoes when his head snapped back and peered straight into her eyes. "What, what do you mean Jack?"

39

"OK Uncle, maybe I need to add some other details to what I've already told you."

Jack then summed up the rest of the story with the Chinatown incident, her shadow Caddie tagalong and the Asian driver. After listening to Jack telling the rest of her story, Uncle Mike stood up and walked over to the fireplace and then turned towards where Jack was sitting.

"Jack, this is serious business. You cannot just go around thinking that Barcelino is not involved in these three separate events. They are connected I am sure. However, I've got my hands tied, and I cannot just call the precinct to have this Dago picked up. He's got deep connections inside the Sheriff's Department and the LAPD. It's a tough case, and we will need solid proof to put this Italian Kingpin away for good."

"Uncle," Jack pleaded, "Don't do anything until I have had a couple of days to look around. I need to find out what's at stake here. How deep Donnie is and where does Barcelino fit into all of this. Just a couple of days, then you can do as you please."

"Alright," Uncle Mike responded, "But only if I have one of my men follow you."

"OK," Jack responded, "But only if he wears civvies. I don't want him spotted by whoever is following me."

Uncle Mike nodded his head and walked to the phone and dialed the squad room at his precinct.

As Jack walked to the kitchen to get a glass of water, she heard her Uncle talk to someone called Gary. When he completed his conversation, he walked into the kitchen smiling.

Jack looked at him and asked, "Is that anyone I know?"

With a grin on his face, he said, "Perhaps."

Jack smiled back as her Uncle explained. "Gary was due for retirement anyway, and though the Marines wanted to keep him in for the duration of the War, they also thought that he could do just as much service if he were attached stateside and working for us. So, the Marines are paying his salary, but he's under my jurisdiction, for the duration, and you must follow his lead."

Jack smiled again both inwardly and outwardly, knowing that Gary would once again be by her side. She and Gary had just gotten done chasing down Carmen Ialucci and the Mancini Family, so this would be perfect. She was feeling quite safe and contented when she fell asleep that evening, knowing that she would be in some good company pursuing the ruthless Barcelino.

Music is Life…and Death
Chapter 7

In the morning while Aunt Dorothy was making breakfast, both Jack and her Uncle read the newspaper and commented from time to time about who and what was happening.

Unemployment was almost zero, due to the War effort, though many jobs were now being completed by women since their boyfriends and husbands were overseas.

Thinking to herself Jack noted, "Perhaps this was why it was easier for the Mafia to carve out territories throughout the United States."

As much as we didn't want their involvement, the government used the Mob in almost every major city, and they used the local powers, including the police and other agencies for their political purpose. It was hard to stick anything on anyone unless they were caught killing someone outright.

The FBI was stretched thin throughout the country but mainly on both coasts where they managed the Mafia Families as much as they could along with hundreds of Sabotage investigations.

The Mafia acted as a roadblock to the Germans invading America, but occasionally either from oversight, payoffs or just some damn luck "Gerry or Fritz" would sneak someone into the country.

The fear that extended from the top down was that these infiltrators would blow up something or someone important. It was a game of checkers between America,

Japan, and Germany. And locally it was just as tense, between rival families, like the various Italians Clans and Chinese Tong.

The FBI also monitored the Hollywood and New York writers for film and songwriters for music, since many had strong ties to the Communist Party. For the writers it was all about their share of the profits and the Mob played both sides to make sure they got their cut.

Studio Chiefs, in particular, had concerns about the unions, not just because of the Mob but the influence over everything they controlled.

Along with the strange bedroom relationship the Government had with some of the Mafia Families, even stranger was the New York and Hollywood Studios and entertainment companies and agencies. The Chicago Outfit, as it was named was allegedly involved and controlled quite of few Studios, and so it came as no surprise that they would muscle into the Music Business since several of the Movie Studios were forming or in control of the recording side of that enterprise.

In New York, Decca, Columbia, and Victor were the big three Recording Companies. It was hard to say if they had been infiltrated and how legit all three were, but for the moment, Jack needed to concentrate on Donnie Heaven and his contract with Barcelino.

As Jack came to find out, Uncle Mike had assisted the Feds and tried to put the ring around a crime boss by the name of Jack Dragna, but for some reason, Captain O'Keefe kept running aground with his leads. Even the Families fought against each other, so it was an uneasy marriage between friend and foe alike, and sometimes you didn't know who was who!

"However impossible," said Uncle Mike, "if we could tie the killing yesterday back to Dragna or Barcelino, then this time we could close down another crime syndicate in Los Angeles for sure.

Besides one small paragraph on the murder of Dick Linsky, the gossip column in the papers and celebrity news on the radio was all about the new movie that was scheduled to be out shortly. They kept moving its release date back, but Yankee Doodle Dandy, starring Jimmy Cagney, was sure to be a hit no matter when they released it.

Another piece in the paper dealt with the ongoing retaliation between the "Zoot Suits" (Mexican Americans) and the Sailors that had started back in March. It seemed that every time they were in the near vicinity of each other, a fist fight would flare up. Jack asked her Uncle if this had happened up in the Hollywood area, where his precinct was, and he said, "No, but then you never know with the Hollywood Canteen just opening."

After some more chit chat, Jack took a shower and got dressed for the day. She had arranged that Gary and herself meet publicly for lunch at a famous restaurant on Hollywood Boulevard so that whoever was tailing her would know that she had some muscle with her.

"Musso and Frank" was part of the golden age of Hollywood, where the who's who attended the daily drink and dine fest. It is a known fact that from the '20s through '42 waiters had served many stars and writers including Pickford and Garbo. Tough guys like Edward G. Robinson and Cesar Romero drank their scotch and gin regularly, and the back room became a home away from home to Fitzgerald, Falkner, and Hemingway to name a few.

Charlie Chaplin frequented the restaurant more than any other place in town. Cooper and Rogers enjoyed the cuisine as well. And Valentino and Fairbanks became regular customers hanging out till wee hours when they closed the joint!

Many writers who were in the know settled into the Hollywood lifestyle and received bigger paychecks from the studios, because of the talent agencies, than from their books.

Raymond Chandler mentioned the restaurant in his novel, "The Big Sleep."

The stories of the restaurant could have been more myth than legend, but the fact that anyone who was anybody seemed to be there either boozing it up or dining was real. Contracts and terminations seemed to take place in the back room. Studio execs and Mob members were intertwined, and so most of what you heard had to hold some truth to the legends.

Even overzealous fans or photographers were never allowed to bother or interfere with the celebrities and diners at the well-known restaurant. Privacy and its food were world famous.

Around noon, Jack pulled Big Red into the back-parking lot of the restaurant. It was already busy, as the valet took her keys and tipped his hat as she placed her blue velvet high heels onto the pavement, dressed in her midnight blue cotton pants and white Mandarin neckline blouse. She noticed the lot had several limos and large sedans parked with the drivers waiting. Entering the front door, she was quite surprised to find only a few tables and chairs filled with customers. Ah, she thought, the famous "Back Room." She wondered who was back there today!

The maître d', Romano, smiled as Jack walked up to him and told him a "Table for two." He told her to follow him, and they proceeded to a table in a front corner that looked towards the door but could also see everyone else who came out of the back room.

"May I get anything for the lady, while she is waiting?", the maître d' asked.

"Yes, coffee with cream" Jack replied.

"Right away" Romeo answered in his broken English and rushed off.

As she scanned the restaurant, occasionally the door to the "back room" would open and she would hear several loud voices. It was hard to tell what was being said or by whom, so she just waited for her sidekick.

Gary was never late, but today, he was about fifteen minutes past due, when the door opened, and he motioned to Jack as he passed the maître d'. As usual, the "Jarhead" was dressed fashionably well in a grey suit and an open white collared shirt, along with a white handkerchief poking out of the top left pocket.

Kissing her on the left cheek, he said, "I'm sorry Jack for the tardiness. I couldn't get here any sooner since your Uncle wanted to make sure that I was up to par before I came barreling over here."

"Ah, you stopped by the precinct?" Jack asked.

Gary smiled and responded. "No, it was more like, be here at 10:15 sharp so that we can go over the game plan, per your Uncle!"

Jack laughed and told him, "No problem, my Uncle was just a little more cautious this time because of the possible Barcelino or criminal connection."

After they ordered lunch, Jack updated Gary on everything she knew. She mentioned that there was one thing that she couldn't figure out, "What was so important about this particular songwriter and his contract to a Mob member?"

Gary took a moment and said, "Jack, maybe it's more than just a song or a simple contract. Perhaps it's the person involved or a contract for a person's life. You know the Mob; if they think they can make money, then you are connected to them forever, not just for a song."

Jack looked at Gary and smiled, then said, "That's it! Donnie must be up to his eyebrows with Barcelino. And Donnie was looking to find a way out. That's why there is only his name on these documents and no one else."

Gary stated, "We need to get to Donnie. Talk to him about his deal. It could be life or death for him, and whoever else is involved with his plans to start that record label."

They were finishing their lunch and conversation, when the door to the Back Room opened and out came Joey Barcelino, along with several of his bodyguards and a very famous actor.

Every man was dressed superbly in suits, mostly "sharkskin" which was fitting for their personality. (Sharkskin Fabric usually came from Italy and South America and had been around since the 1800s. The original version included a Worsted Wool with silk mixed into the weave. It's considered lightweight, wrinkle-free and worn in any climate. Because of the tight weave and thread count, it has a sheen to the texture of the cloth and appearance. Hence the name was coined to that of the common shark).

As they walked past their table to stand in front of the doors, Jack could not take her eyes off them. Then Barcelino turned and looked at Jack straight in her eyes. He took a breath, wheezed and then asked, "Girl, haven't you ever seen a movie star before?"

Jack almost panicked, but calmly responded with, "It's not that, I just haven't been around this many handsome men since my prom!"

Everyone laughed, while Gary just stared at Jack wondering.

After that they all turned and walked out the door, with the famous actor, bowing slightly to Jack. After they all left, Jack said to Gary, "That was Barcelino?"

Gary responded, "What, I thought you told me that you hadn't met him?"

"I hadn't," Jack smiled, "But it just so happened this morning I saw his picture in the L.A. Times. Lucky for me I now have had an up close and personal meeting with an L.A. Syndicate King."

Gary snickered, "If only he knew it was you?"

Jack cautiously smiled and said, "Yeah, he'd have one of his thugs take me outside..."

It was about 2:15 when Gary and Jack left. She had asked Gary to go back to the precinct to see if he could dig up some more information on Donnie and his partners.

Jack told Gary that she was going to visit her old newspaper buddy, Brad Davis. Perhaps Brad could shed some light on who the guests were in the "Back Room" at Musso and Frank.

Jack also hoped that Brad could tell her how or where the famous actor and Joey Barcelino fit together since they were hanging out in such a public place.

Gary and Jack agreed to meet up towards 7 in the evening at another well-known restaurant, called Formosa Café. Going to the Formosa was a way to be where the action might be and a good place to find out more about Barcelino and his gang.

Music is Life…and Death
Chapter 8

Dick Linsky's house sat overlooking Hollywood in the Hollywood Hills. Sitting opposite yet in plain view was the "Hollywoodland" sign located on Mount Lee, where Harry Chandler, publisher of the Los Angeles Times and landowner, had invested into its development.

Linsky's house was the scene of many parties for the Hollywood crowd that no doubt included some of the more infamous criminal members.

During the War, from New York to Hollywood, the "Family" now controlled several entertainment businesses, where much of their money came from, outside of collaboration with the government to control the ports.

Most "Families" controlled one or two areas, like gambling and prostitution. In the case of Barcelino, he was a major crime boss in Hollywood, urged by Chicago to keep watch over the up and coming gambling casinos in the desert town of Las Vegas, besides the "gaming clubs" in Palm Springs.

Barcelino also controlled several movie studios, actors and singers and governed the radio shows and much of what was played over the air, by using independent promotion men.

These men, who traveled in twos and threes, would go to a station and tell the promotion or music director what to play and how many times a day to play it. Then they would give the director money, cars, dames or even a house, as the pay-off for their support.

Because of the War, there was little national or state control in the entertainment business because the Feds and the local Police didn't have enough resource agents or officers to patrol it. So, at best they could only try to keep a lid on it, so it didn't blow up and become a public eyesore. No one knew that when they heard Billie Thomas's Big Band or Donnie Heaven singing on the radio that it was likely because of one of the "Families" forced the station to play it. Nor did the public realize that they were themselves programmed what music they did hear.

Linsky's house was just off Nichols Canyon. It was a large two-storied house, with over 6000 square feet, a pool, cabana, four car garage, and a tennis court. It encompassed six bedrooms and adjoining bathrooms, two kitchens, a wine cellar and a small office upstairs. Most of the stars from Hollywood and New York at one time or another had stayed there, either by choice or because they were too drunk to drive home.

Linsky had been a star for nearly twenty years who gained popularity out of the old silent picture days. His voice was a strong yet English gruff sound with polished American slang. Born to a Connecticut family from England, he was first generation American.

Driving up from Hollywood Boulevard, Sergeant O'Shay arrived with another patrol car. They drove up a single gravel road that led them past the gardens into a circular driveway.

O'Shay rang the doorbell then he and four police officers waited several minutes before the door opened.

"Dressed to the nines" in his semi black and grey tux suit stood the butler. O'Shay showed the butler his badge and asked him to please have the entire house attendants meet with him regarding the death of Mr. Linsky. The butler looked confused but did as he was told motioning for the officers to come inside, as he led them into the drawing room. He then disappeared through the doorway to fetch the rest of the house staff.

After ten minutes, six of the staff members assembled, including the butler, the driver, and four housemaids.

O'Shay looked at the residence document that he had obtained from police records and said, "There seems to be one staff member missing? I have a sheet that says that seven members work here. Missing is Mr. Koto. Kim Koto. Does anyone know where he is today?"

The butler looked at O'Shay and said in his very proper English accent, "It's Mr. Koto's day off! He is the gardener but once a week has a day to go into town".

O'Shay was not happy with the answer, but said, "We need to talk to him, so when he gets back, please ask him to call the precinct to speak with me."

The butler nodded, and O'Shay proceeded to inform the staff of what had happened and that they would all be required to give statements to the officers and then they would have to find other locations to live and work. But for now, none of them were allowed to leave Los Angeles and needed to keep the police informed of their whereabouts.

The Sergeant went on to say that they had three days to find other employment as the house was now the property of the police and would remain so until the investigation was over.

O'Shay and another officer went about examining the house, while the other two policemen, took down information from the staff.

Upstairs, O'Shay and his fellow officer were a bit amused looking through Linsky's closets and dresser drawers, adjacent to his bedroom. They found large amounts of money rolled up and held together by rubber bands, everywhere throughout the bedroom area.

Stuffed under a stack of sweaters, they found a manila envelope with a contract signed by Joey Barcelino. In it, was stated that Dick would carry documents to New York to meet with another member of the Salvatore Family at any given time that was required. The contract also indicated Linsky's agreement with one of the major movie studios but was with Barcelino and not with the studio itself.

One last disturbing document was a hand-written letter that directed Linsky to get Donnie Heaven to sign the agreement with Barcelino or else!

O'Shay surmised that Linsky might have been the target after all and not accidentally murdered. The Sergeant thought that with his dealings with the Barcelino organization, they would not have wanted to bring the cops down on themselves.

Barcelino might have only wanted to scare Linsky and ultimately Donnie Heaven. Unfortunately, it didn't turn out that way.

Meanwhile, the two police officers who were taking statements found out that the driver was a man called Mickey Bucco from Sicily. Standing still, the butler spoke up for Mickey since he spoke terrible English and was sweating profusely.

Continuing their questioning of the Staff, the officers were able to find out that Mickey was employed by the Barcelino Family, while the English butler, George Tumbly was originally an employee of the Salvatore Family in New York but was transferred to L.A. so the New York Family could keep track of Linsky.

The four maids werc just locales from a maid service, that happened to be owned by Barcelino. The officers got the impression after interviewing the attendants that none of them seemed to be involved in the death of Linsky, except for maybe the driver, so they informed O'Shay of their findings.

That afternoon the cops placed many items that they collected along with the money in evidence bags. O'Shay had lots of information for Captain O'Keefe to look at but was troubled about the gardener, being away the day that Linsky got gunned down and of the sweating driver.

Later that afternoon, Gary met with Captain O'Keefe and Sergeant O'Shay to find out more about Dick Linsky and hopefully Donnie Heaven.

Having turned all the evidence over to the lab, O'Shay completed his briefing to his boss and the Marine. The gardener was still missing, and no one could seem to locate him, so the Sergeant put an APB out on Koto.

Then the Captain told Gary what they had found out about Randy Winter, the young man killed in Chinatown.

Randy was 21 years of age who was 4-F for the military so that he couldn't join any of the services. His lungs were not good. Somewhere along his path he connected with Donnie, and they hit it off, so he was employed by Mr. Heaven as a driver, runner, doing various errands. More times than not during the day, Donnie would have Randy drive around Hollywood, to deliver and pick up things, as requested. Donnie paid him a pretty good salary, and soon he had met May Ling at a party that Donnie had given at his home, and May was one of the "ladies" who were available for the night to the guests.

Donnie's driver had arranged for the Asian women through his connections, and so Donnie never knew that May was part of Mr. Chung's organization.

Gary was surprised that Randy would hire girls from Chung's organization, but then who would the Barcelino associate have gone to for supplying Chinese women? And wouldn't this put both Families in bed together?

The Captain mentioned to Gary that he might want to check with Jack and her contacts regarding what type of arrangement the two Families had? After that, the two men called it a day.

As decided, Jack drove to downtown to the L.A. paper to visit with old pal Brad. She wanted to know what exactly took place at Musso and Frank's "Back Room" and if Brad heard anything about Randy Winter and Donnie Heaven.

Brad was full of information that Jack could not have imagined. He told her that Randy, the murdered man, and Donnie might have been lovers.

The occasional Hollywood hookup amongst an older man and younger guy was prevalent amongst the Tinsel Town men who were bi-sexual.

There were rumors of many famous stars being that way. At several of Donnie's parties, some intimacies had to be covered up to not upset the studio bosses and their stockholders, let alone the public.

Brad told Jack that there was one studio head who was a frequent guest of the Donnie Heaven estate that reportedly was found in the arms of another star on more than one occasion.

Brad went on to say that the Hollywood Women were not left out in the cold on sharing themselves with their bi-sexual lovers either, and in some circles and nightly parties had sex with other starlets, both old and new.

It was a truly swinging "tinsel" town. It was Hollywood where almost anything was possible and plausible at any time. Women, Men, booze and drugs; it was all part of the game of stardom, corruption, crime and the underworld, and who controlled who.

Music is Life….and Death
Chapter 9

Brad kept showing Jack pictures of the Crime Bosses coming and going into various restaurants throughout Los Angeles. Most of the pictures were taken by the police, FBI or by some "photo junky" that loved taking candid pictures of gangsters smiling, brooding or caught in the moment.

Soon Jack's head was spinning like a bottle cap, so she pushed away from the clippings and sat back in her chair and just looked at Brad.

Brad smiled and said, "Pretty scary stuff. Knowing that we all live amidst this chaos and yet most of the populace only know what they read or hear on the radio and if it doesn't affect them directly then they ignore it, like a disease. The cops only keep a lid on it because the government needs these bad guys to help control our enemies at bay.

Sometimes the balance of power shifts and the authorities must take real action against the same people they use to secure our borders. It's a messy life no matter if it's during war or peace."

Jack knew that Brad was right. She had seen it repeatedly, even when her Dad was alive. Everyone used each other to gain something. And yes, it was just like a "jack in a box," as you played the music you knew that eventually, the jack would pop up, but you didn't know when.

Believing that life was the same, Jack knew that with every straight line there was a curve or corner, but you never knew when and what was around that bend.

Leaving Brad to go meet up with Gary, she was feeling a little depressed. Even though Brad had given her some good information, it didn't help her tie any loose ends together, so she hoped that Gary would have something more tangible.

When she finally got to the restaurant, it was closer to 7:30. Gary had gotten there just before 7, so he had a good start on Jack, drinking his cocktail.

Walking up behind Gary, Jack chuckled as she came and sat next to him. Gary was busy at the bar chit chatting with a good looking blonde waitress and the bartender. Though the Formosa was mildly busy, it was like he was holding court at the bar and the blonde certainly was interested in whatever he was saying.

Gary hadn't noticed Jack until she leaned over and kissed him on the cheek and said, "I'm sorry darling for being so late. I hope you missed me because I missed you!" Jack then did something uncanny for her as she looked down and grabbed his left leg just below his family jewels.

The waitress looked at Jack in shock and just turned and walked away in a huff. Jack started to laugh as did Gary.

The bartender just shook his head and walked to the other end of the bar to attend to another patron.

Gary then said, "You broke up my chance of getting lucky tonight. I was on a roll!"

Jack smiled then replied, "If I am not getting any, then neither are you!"

They both laughed, and Jack motioned for the bartender to bring her a glass of Chardonnay, as they moved to a table nearby.

Discussing what they had learned, it was educational but not enough to go after anyone at that point.

Agreeing to visit Chung, they hoped to learn more about the arrangement between the two Families. It bothered Jack that it was possible that Chung might have benefited from Donnie Heaven contracted for life with Barcelino. But money was to be made in the world of the Families, no matter what race they were.

In their conversation, Gary and Jack had several major concerns that Barcelino might be putting the squeeze on music companies along with the movie studios, while the authorities looked the other way. Given the War effort and the lack of surveillance on the regular side of life, it was no wonder that the Families could get into a company and take it over. There was just no recourse at this stage.

Gary told Jack that the missing gardener concerned him deeply. He said that the police could track the staff from the house, except for Kim Koto. Because he was Japanese, it was harder to find out who he was and where he came from. The only possible link was that several of the patrons at the Bombay told the police that the man was standing in the door with a "Tommy gun" looked Asian. Could it be that the Italians had hired Koto to do some of their dirty work?

Jack was perplexed. The story seemed to go everywhere and that a lot of different people were involved with the Mob along with Barcelino, in running of the entertainment side that came out of Hollywood.

No one seemed to know how and where Koto came from during these war years. To have a Japanese person work for you would have required some sort of waiver since most of the Japanese had been rounded up and placed in American internment camps throughout the U.S.

Jack told Gary that in her discussion with Brad, he had informed her about Columbia Studios and the current movies being filmed there and who all the lyricists were for the soundtracks.

The funny thing was that Donnie Heaven was in the running for writing the songs for one of the movies that Rita Hayworth was starring in, but Mercer seemed to be the celebrity star at that moment and had gotten the contract. Had Barcelino been muscling his way into Columbia? No, because Harry Cohn had his own connections to Chicago, as Brad told Jack, so Columbia wasn't having any problems financially or otherwise.

As Jack thought, "Perhaps that's why Heaven never got the OK to write for Columbia – conflicting participation amongst Mob Families. Cohn told Chicago that he was pissed off at being muscled by Barcelino, so Lansky told Mickey Cohen to have a chat with Barcelino."

Also, Brad told Jack about Johnny Mercer and his new Record Label, Capitol Records. It all seemed to mirror what Donnie was trying to do or vice versa, with one exception and that was that Barcelino wanted in to control it.

Mercer and Heaven were the two biggest songwriters in the music and movie business in '42.

Both had performed together for the troops on several occasions. They were acquaintances, but not the best of friends. Their cronies and friends were a different crowd. Heaven hung out with the wild drinking, partying type and Mob associates. A noted bi-sexual, it was said that Donnie had been Dick Linsky's lover for many years. Of course, the public relations firms for both men denied any rumors surrounding this bit of news.

Digesting it all, Gary and Jack decided that it was essential to go back to Chung's to revisit the connection and figure out where the Asian came into the picture. Plus the importance of Mickey Bucco since he worked for Barcelino and the girls were supplied from Chung. There had to be more to the story than what Chung had already told them.

Jack asked Gary to go to Linsky's house in the morning and snoop around to find out what else he could about Mickey Bucco; who he was and where would he and the rest of the Linsky's staff move to, now that the police controlled the house.

After eating the chicken fried rice, Jack walked over to the bar and asked to use the phone. It was nearly 9 PM when she called Jimmy Woo and asked if it was too late to see Mr. Chung? Jimmy said he would call to find out and would call her right back.

Jack then told Jimmy where she was and gave him the number and hung up the phone.

Gary was finishing his Mongolian beef when the phone rang, and the bartender motioned for Jack that it was for her. Walking over to the bar she took the phone from the bartender and listened.

Jimmy said it would be OK to see Chung and asked her how long it would take her to get to his office.

Jack looked at her blue dial Cartier watch that her Dad had given her on her 21st birthday and said, "Give us twenty minutes!"

With that, Jimmy said, "OK" and hung up.

Picking up their things and the check, to meet with Chung, Gary paid the bill and asked the bartender if it was OK to leave his car in the lot for another few hours. The bartender told him OK, but that the bar closed at 2 am, and he needed the car gone by then. Gary said it would and followed Jack through the doors of the restaurant to Jack's car.

The night air in L.A. was sometimes sweet. On this night, it smelled like hibiscus. "Perhaps it's just my imagination," Jack thought, "but I swear that I had smelled that before?" But for the moment she couldn't remember where or when.

Driving Big Red to Chung's, Gary and Jack chatted about life avoiding the case. Jack kept tabs on her rearview mirror, and Gary kept turning around to look as well. To their surprise, they had no one following them.

Even though Jack had begun to cherish the fact that someone was always following her, tonight was different. She felt naked and strange without her sinister companions and kept waiting for the other "shoe to drop," and out of the darkness, the Caddie would reappear. But nothing happened, and they arrived at Chung's unmolested and unharmed.

Jimmy was there to greet them as Jack swung the car into the oval parking lot. He told Jack to leave the keys in the car in case they had to move it, so Gary and Jack both got out of the car and walked inside the building with Jimmy leading the way.

Chung's office was mostly westernized but with Asian artifacts all around. Rosewood and teak furniture and several shoji screens were interspersed around the room with the Chung Red Dragon logo placed purposely in unmistakably visible spots.

Chung sat at a huge desk made of the same wood. Tonight he was dressed in a simple short-sleeved Chinese linen purple jacket with a Red Dragon embroidered on the left side and matching pants, he stood out in the room. He got up from his chair when they all entered and came over to reach out his hand to shake hands with each one of them.

Jack was impressed with his openness because every other time before it was, she who bowed before starting a conversation. "What changed," She thought?

Looking deep into his eyes Jack said, "Thank you, Mr. Chung, and thank you for seeing us on such short notice."

He responded by saying, "Jack, I am sure that your appointment is urgent; otherwise you would not have requested this meeting, so late in the night?"

Jack said, "Yep, you are so right!"

"Please sit down, won't you?" Chung stated.

Sitting on the oversized red sofa centered in the room, Chung sat down opposite to them on a curved out teak chair with a red padded cushion.

As soon as they were all seated Jack blurted out, "Mr. Chung, we have found out that Mickey Bucco had been the go-between your organization and Barcelino to supply the women for the parties and social events held by Dick Linsky. That said, how does the Italian family hire these girls from the Chinese family and how is it that the Italians have an Asian working for them?"

Chung was not unnerved by these questions but simply said, "Jack, it's business. When Barcelino requested the girls, it was only natural for us to supply them, since we are the only business in Chinatown. It's all about money. We had no other reason, and we weren't involved with anything else that the Italians might be into. We kept it very simple: the girls for cash and nothing more!"

"But what about the Asian?" Jack asked.

Chung remained calm and said, "I am most distressed by the news of someone who was thought to be of our ancestry, has gunned down an important celebrity and has the backing of Barcelino. I have recently come into this information that connects Bucco, Kim Koto and Barcelino, and I am not happy about it. Though I must tell you that Kim is not Chinese but Japanese, so he is not under our umbrella."

Chung continued, "Kim Koto was orphaned but raised by a respected Italian Family in South Los Angeles. Before the War, while he was in High School, he joined an Italian gang since they were outcasts in the community of

Germans and Jews. Ultimately this relationship led him to Mickey Bucco and then to Barcelino.

Jack stood up and took a few steps from the couch and said, "So then this is all Barcelino's doing?"

"Yes," responded Chung. "We have nothing to gain in his endeavors for power over the Hollywood crowd. Nor do I think that we could ever be granted that type of access since we are Asian. There is still the ever-present racism and discrimination that stretches from the Jews to the Whites and Blacks and the "Orientals" and our natural races to mistrust each other, so there is no way that we could ever control the studios without causing the government to get involved."

Jack knew what Chung was saying. She had to agree.

Moving slightly forward on the couch, Gary said to Chung, "Do you know how we can find Bucco or Koto?"

Chung replied, "They were both working at Linsky's, but I have heard that they have vanished, so we are out looking for them ourselves, particularly because of the incident with May Ling. We believe that Koto was the connection and the cause for the death of Randy Winter."

With that, Jack thanked Chung and told him that they would be in touch.

As the three left the office, Jimmy asked Jack, "Did you think that Chung was involved with Barcelino?"

"Yes, but I didn't know how deep so I had to make sure" Jack replied.

"Ok," said Jimmy, "But you have to give Chung more credit than that. He is straightforward and on your side. He doesn't want to upset the apple cart, because if he did the authorities would be all over Chinatown."

Jack smiled at Jimmy and said, "Alright, I get it now. I am sorry if I doubted him, but now I know for sure. Thanks, Jimmy."

As Gary and Jack got back into the Buick, it was nearly 11 PM. Both were bushed and only wanted to get some sleep, so Jack put Big Red into gear and started to drive back to the restaurant to pick up Gary's car.

Jack asked Gary, "Where are you staying for the night?"

Gary said, "Don't know, thought I'd just cruise the boulevard till one of those cheap ass motels popped up along the road."

Jack laughed. "No, tonight is on me. Follow me after you get your car. I am calling in a marker or should I say a favor for the night."

After Gary got his car, they drove over to the Hollywood Roosevelt Hotel. Named after Theodore Roosevelt, it was situated in the middle of Hollywood and was originally financed by a group that included Douglas Fairbanks, Mary Pickford, and Louis B. Mayer. It opened its doors on 15 May 1927, and had since become a fashionable place to stay. Though there was always rumbling about ghosts, Jack had never experienced one in all her times she had stayed there. Hopefully, tonight would be no different.

Unbeknownst to Jack, Gary knew the Manager of the hotel as he had been stationed with Jack's Dad when he was in the Navy. So when they got to the hotel and walked up to the front desk, Jack asked to see Tommy Thorngood. Gary looked at Jack surprised and said, "Hell, I didn't know you knew Tommy?"

"Why of course I do silly," Jack said.

Retired due to some shrapnel in his right leg, Tommy came limping out from behind the windowed wall with a smile on his face as he moved to the counter to greet his old friends. Happy to see them both, he told the night clerk to assign a couple of suites for his special guests.

Tommy and Gary then started talking all about Navy stuff, and Jack pouted and waited till the night clerk gave her a key, then said, "Good night Boys. I'll catch up with you later and Thanks, Tommy."

Tommy smiled, "Anytime," then he kissed Jack on the cheek and turned back to Gary to continue their conversation.

Jack was barely able to brush her teeth and climb into bed when her mind shut off and she was fast asleep.

In Brentwood, pacing in his home, Barcelino met with Koto and Mickey Bucco.

There Joey told them both to clean up the loose ends and go back to Chinatown and find May Ling and the missing documents.

They were told to then drive to Linsky's and look for anything that might tie Dick to Joey. Barcelino didn't want anything linking him to the murder.

Mickey informed Joey what the cops had told the staff at Linsky's and Joey responded gruffly, "Don't worry about it, we have people in places that will silence the cops from interfering."

Then the three devised a plan to abduct May Ling and to take care of Donnie's partners.

Music is Life…and Death
Chapter 10

Like Johnny Mercer and friends Glenn Wallichs and Buddy
DeSylva, Donnie Heaven wanted to establish a record
company that would pave the way for his songs and for the
new talent that was being discovered during the '40s.
However, Barcelino wanted to control it and Donnie.

Mercer and his partners, record retailer Wallichs, (owned
Music City), and Paramount Pictures' DeSylva, had already
opened Liberty Records for business on April 8, 1942.
(Later the name was changed to Capitol Records).

Donnie was watching their every move and knew that he
could replicate it and be just as successful. He just wanted
to do it his way.

It seemed that between the War, since there was a lack of
shellac for records and the AFM strike, it may have been
the worst time to start a record company and try to record
new music, but in spite of these things Mercer was able to
roll out the records, under the new label moniker.

Furthermore, other records companies that existed during
this time included Paramount Records (founded during the
1910s in Wisconsin), made reissues of historical recordings
along with new recordings of jazz and blues artists.

On the East Coast, there was Decca (originally formed in
Britain), and other labels RCA Victor and Columbia, as
well as R&B (Rhythm and Blues) record companies:
Savoy, De Luxe, Apollo, and National.

Musicians wages and lifestyles had changed over the years,
and it didn't matter whether you were white or black.

Studios, either recording or film, controlled most of the money-making opportunities unless you were fortunate to still make money from traveling or famous enough to be paid a substantial salary from a club owner.

Donnie was so far in debt to Barcelino that he knew that he would probably never get out from under his control. No matter what he planned to do, Barcelino would always be taking 50% of everything he earned. So, it left little money to get Donnie into the black. Hence, Donnie believed that he had to establish a new record company without Joey, to have the ability to become a major star and owner of a record company like Mercer.

The contract for the new record company called Velvet Tone Records and the new songs that Randy Winter was supposed to deliver to Donnie's partners respectively had only made it to May Ling's apartment. Somehow, Barcelino had found out from Dick Linsky that Bebop and Alan had agreed to front the money needed to establish this new endeavor and that Joey was not to be part of the deal.

Enraged, Barcelino threatened to kill Donnie for trying to cut him out of any deal, especially since Donnie still owed him $150,000 plus 25% interest.

One of Donnie's partners, Alan Glass, was a respected Los Angeles attorney, who worked for studios, actors and songwriters. Unfortunately, this placed him in direct line of many of the mob figures, even if he did not approve of them. It was the entertainment business, so no matter where he turned, he would be negotiating with criminals or shady business executives in his line of work.

Alan had been around since the age of the silent screen era, arranging for fair wages for all his clients. As an elder member of a sometimes, outrageous Hollywood crowd, he'd seen at least most of it. But this afternoon, two of Barcelino's thugs had come to his office, ransacked it and knocked the old attorney around. They demanded that Donnie sign the contract or the three of them would pay dearly for not complying.

With this first stop that Koto and Mickey Bucco made, it was at the offices of Alan Glass. The secretary informed them that he was on the phone discussing negotiations of a contract with ASA with another singer.

The two waited about fifteen minutes before being allowed to enter the office. Alan looked surprised as they almost charged through the door. Mickey started to speak, but because of his stutter, he had just begun when Koto edged in front of him and said, "Mr. Glass, you will not sign the contract with Donnie Heaven, and we want to make sure that Donnie only signs the contract with Mr. Barcelino, unless you wish to die!"

Alan, in shock, stood up and said, "I have no idea what you are talking about."

Koto snickered and continued, "Mr. Glass, I am delivering this message directly from Mr. Barcelino that you will jeopardize your health if you sign any contract with Donnie."

Alan began to sweat profusely, then said, "How dare you come into my office and threaten me. I run a respectable business and don't take kindly to anyone else telling me what I can or cannot do!"

As Alan struggled to discuss the situation, he realized it didn't matter what he said. The two thugs only demanded what Joey instructed to say to the old lawyer.

Smirking, Koto said, "Really, I hope you reconsider?"

By the end of the invasion into his office, Alan found himself tied up and had been punched in his face, apparently blacking out from it. When he managed to wake up, he was only able to whisper "help," calling out to his secretary.

Unaware to Alan, Norma had left the building while the thugs were in his office to run to the post office and make two deliveries to the studios. So, no one heard Alan wench in pain, as he tried to move the chair closer to his desk, where he saw the letter opener. Fortunately, there was a small knife encased inside the opener.

After a few minutes, Alan was able to slide his chair right alongside the front of the desk and leaned to one side to grab the opener in his left hand.

Once setting the chair back down, he was then able to push the bottom of the silver handle, and the tiny knife appeared.

After moving the knife in an upright position, he used both hands to start cutting the rope. But then he heard the outer door to his offices open, and someone was walking towards his door. Afraid to say anything at first, he then decided to go ahead and yell out.

The screech that came out of Alan's office scared Norma so much that she crutched down and began to back out of the office. But then she heard almost a cry and stood straight up and walked directly into Alan's office.

Alan's office was dark, and it seemed odd for such a sound coming out of the office, so Norma was careful as she walked up to the door and switched the lights on and saw the dapper gentleman, tied up and struggling with the knife. His face was extremely red and bruised with blood across his mouth.

He looked at her and begun to sob. She ran to him and held him for a minute before taking the opener and slicing the rope open to free his arms and legs.

Norma helped Alan to his feet and said, "You look pretty bad. Should we take you to the hospital?"

Alan grunted and said, "Yes, my face is all numb."

Locking their office, Norma then led Alan past the outer office, to the elevator.

Once outside the building, Norma flagged down a taxi from the corner, and when they were inside the cab, she told the driver, "Metro Hospital and step on it!"

Later that night, after the doctors patched up Alan, Norma called Donnie at his house and woke him up. It was almost 1:30 AM. Besides being Alan's major client, he was also his friend, so Norma thought that Donnie needed to know what had happened.

In shock, Donnie said, "Will he be alright?"

Norma replied, "Yes, but he will have to take it easy for a couple of days."

Donnie thanked Norma for calling him and told her that he would visit Alan in the morning.

That night Donnie decided to go to the police in the morning for help since two of his lovers had been murdered, and now his attorney had been roughed up. He knew he would need help and protection from Barcelino, particularly if he ever wanted to be free of his grip.

Music is Life…and Death
Chapter 11

Extortion was one of the biggest rackets amongst the "entertainment business," that included movie studios, actors, singers, night clubs and music.

The "Chicago Outfit," had been linked to James Petrillo, a previous trombone player in the Paul Whiteman band, was now the leader of the American Federation of Musicians. Jimmy grew up in Chicago's West Side, and violence did not intimidate him. At 5'6" he was a stocky street fighter.

This trade union was for professional musicians, but Jimmy ruled it with an iron fist over the musicians, and anyplace a musician could perform. It posed a major problem for the government since it had yet to wrap its arms around the music industry situation, furthering little interference or control but the Feds. It was like "Prohibition" all over again.

Many up and coming record companies opposed his policies since Petrillo felt that the companies should pay royalties and so he had organized a strike. He wanted to ban union members from all commercial recordings until the record companies started paying royalties.

In the early days, Petrillo's tactics were intimidation. He targeted hotels, theaters and other public locations. In response, he was kidnapped, and his house was bombed. No one was ever convicted, though many were arrested on the possible crime.

Jimmy hated recorded music and thought that a musician would lose money if it were not live music. In spite of his ideas, demands, and detriments, during the early War

Years, some record companies were still able to record and sell records.

Slowly, vinyl material replaced the old 78 rpm (revolutions per minute) shellac records, due to the lack of available material, particularly for the V-Disc records. (short versions – 12 minute or less).

Organized crime had strong ties with major unions throughout America. They included the International Brotherhood of Teamsters (IBT), Hotel and Restaurant Employees Union (HRE), Laborers International Union of North America (Laborers), and International Longshoreman's Association (ILA). Along with this other criminal organizations were instrumental in controlling singers and actors.

Jukeboxes, loansharking, bookmaking, illegal gambling, counterfeiting, prostitution, drug and arms trafficking, smuggling, kidnapping, film studios, and theaters were all susceptible to being controlled by the mobsters. From Meyer Lansky to Bugsy Siegel to Mickey Cohen, there was nowhere that one could hide from racketeering.

Some gangsters married Hollywood stars, while others became friends with presidents of the movie studios. Because the mobsters controlled the unions, many of the studios paid money to the Syndicate to keep their studios running without any labor problems. However, some of the studios reported the attempted shakedown to the cops, but there seemed to be little that could be done to protect them.

Jack Dragna and his organization controlled Southern California and Nevada. However, because of the lack of Italians in the area, Dragna accepted other members from across the country, as directed. With legal horse betting in

Nevada, The Chicago Syndicate sent Bugsy Siegel out to Las Vegas to establish a race wire service. So in the Southwest, control of additional money making opportunities continued to rise.

Dragna also had connections in the Los Angeles Police Department which assisted him in extortion. However, when Siegel came to LA, Dragna resented him from the power that he had in the movie industry.

With Paramount Records being re-activated in 1942, and Capitol Records being established, the idea that new businesses and recordings would flourish without organized crime controlling them particularly during the War years, became the hot item for the Syndicate. However, this was not the case for every record label.

Every imaginable type of music had been recorded since 1900 onto some format. Now reissue labels and new labels sprung up across the country to feed the music hunger: Blues/R&B, country/folk, and jazz. Big bands and singers alike shared in this phenomenon and opportunities.

Mickey Cohen, who reportedly was under the guidance of Bugsy Siegel, ran his own mob-related operation. He owned a nightclub called the "Rhum Boogie" that focused on many R&B acts who were starting their careers but who Mickey controlled. The club was located on Highland Ave, near Hollywood Boulevard.

He was also instrumental in the jukebox operations throughout the Los Angeles area, that gave him a massive amount of money and control over what was called "race" music by owning the artists and the distribution of their music. (R&B music was not normally played on the radio). Though Cohen's actions were at times running cross purposes with the Dragna family, he managed to appease everyone even in the attempts on his life. Barcelino was his friend and enemy at the same time.

Jukebox operation profits were minimal compared to the exploitation of record sales and money laundering. Cohen infiltrated the Hollywood major players throughout the entertainment industry, along with L.A.'s top politicians of the time. Frank Sinatra, Robert Mitchum, Dean Martin, and many more stars paid their homage to Cohen.

Even the Mob went along with Mickey's plan to control a newspaper as well as California's Attorney General.

During the '30s, New York had become the center in its population and the entertainment industry. But by the '40's it had spread across the country.

Meyer Lansky's connection to Mickey Cohen seemed to lean itself to jukebox operations that Mickey controlled in Los Aneles which had started years before in Hallandale Florida, when Lansky and another bookish member of the syndicate, Vincent Alo, bought into Wurlitzer. The cash from the jukeboxes had to be laundered, so they established the Simplex Distribution Company. This new business provided control of popular music outlets, that more than likely allowed singer, Frank Sinatra's career to blossom.

Music is Life…and Death
Chapter 12

The next day, Gary was driving to Linsky's house and drove onto Ivar St., which was called Lysol Alley.

Ironically many of the East Coast actors and writers lived around the area. It was cheap and close to Musso & Frank. The reason why it was called Lysol Alley was that many homeless people also lived on the street and alleyways.

Gary was taking in the cool, foggy morning when he noticed a Black Packard in his rearview mirror. It was about one car length behind him but appeared to be following him. Initially, it didn't bother him until he realized that he was now in the Hollywood Hills area and the car was still behind him.

Trying to second guess who was driving the car, Gary decided to pull over along Nicholas Canyon and stop the car. As soon as he stopped, the Packard turned the corner and was out of sight.

Having second thoughts now, that he might just be spooked or even paranoid, Gary put the car in drive and sped away from the curb and continued to Linsky's.

Upon his arrival, he found that there were no police on duty and no markers to secure the house from the public and the gate was wide open. He didn't believe that the cops would have been relieved of duty so fast, which caused his hairs on the back of his neck to feel like they were straining against his collar.

Driving slowly up the gravel road, he noticed how manicured the lawn was and how the flower beds even in the fog appeared in a ray of color. Peering off into the hills and Mt. Lee above the home he thought, "Sad, that in the end, we leave it all behind us!"

After stopping the car and getting out, he felt the cool air rush against his cheeks, and the smell of roses as the faintest light from the sun shone through the clouds.

Walking up the steps to the front door he turned the handle and walked into the foyer. Unlocked he stood quietly looking at both sides, where large ten foot white and tan marble vases greeted him, and the marble floor sparkled in darker tones of tan and natural brown. To the right stood a white grand piano with one fern plant draping itself over the keys.

Gary yelled out loud, "Hello," but no one answered him. He remembered the last time he walked through another dead man's house – it was eerie, almost scary. There were no sounds, no feeling of life, and a sense of no air.

Looking around he continued to walk throughout the house. He noticed that nothing seemed to be out of place, nor did it look like anyone searched through the house. Walking along what seemed to be a path, Gary began to pick up cushions from the chairs and couch, checking behind the paintings, and lifting the sculptures.

Towards the dining room, he noticed a large framed photograph, rather than a painting. It was of Dick, Donnie, and Barcelino, standing alongside a famous Chicago Outfit man, who was sent to Nevada to set up the betting wire service. It was Bugsy Siegel. A criminal who loved the good life and notoriety. The picture was taken at a golf course someplace in the desert, as all four men were dressed accordingly, in their golf pants, shoes and vests, smiling and leaning on their clubs.

Gary instinctively looked behind the picture and found a safe. Realizing that he didn't have the combination, he just made a mental note to have it opened by an expert.

Walking up the circular stairway, Gary noticed the many pictures aligned the wall of Dick's movies and awards.

From one of the rooms on the second level he thought he heard a noise, and as he rounded the bend to the top of the staircase, he was sure that there was someone in the master bedroom.

Drawing out his revolver, he stepped onto the landing, when Bucco grabbed the gun in Gary's hand. However, Gary swung around with his left fist and punched Bucco directly in the nose.

Stunned Bucco fell backward releasing his hand from the gun and started screaming as he held his nose with both hands.

Looking like Bucco was going to get up and charge at him, Gary smacked Bucco across the face with the gun. With that, the large Italian collapsed on the floor.

By this time, Koto, who had been in the master bedroom, leaped on Gary's back, wrapping his hands around Gary's throat, forcing him to drop his gun.

A bit taller and heavier than Koto, Gary was able to push back as hard as he could, then turned his body, and the two men fell over the hallway glass table, that was against the wall.

At this angle, Gary toppled Koto onto the glass, which broke against Koto's right side. He screamed in pain, releasing his hands from the choke hold, as the shards of glass cut through his clothing.

Gary disengaged himself from Koto, stumbled forward and coughed. His throat ached from the choke hold, but he was able to find his gun and smacked Koto on his forehead to silence his other attacker.

Koto was now knocked out in a pool of blood and Gary didn't care if he were alive or dead. It had been a horrific struggle with Bucco and Koto that Gary wasn't prepared for this morning but was able to overcome nausea settling in.

Staggering into the master bedroom, Gary was trying to adjust himself as he looked for the phone. Hearing some sort of thump coming from the doorway, Gary swung around and found Bucco, all bloodied walking towards him with a knife in his hand.

Gary was still holding his gun and didn't bat an eye as he lifted his right arm and fired twice into Bucco's chest causing the Italian to fall through the doorway. He certainly was now dead.

Feeling no remorse, Gary turned again and found the phone and called the precinct to make his report.

The sergeant of the watch answered the call, and Gary proceeded to tell him who he was and where he was and what had happened. The sergeant then said, "wait there, and I will dispatch a couple of patrol cars immediately."

Gary told the sergeant to notify Captain O'Keefe of the situation pronto, and if possible, come to Linsky's house himself.

After hanging up the phone, Gary decided he needed a drink. Walking to the doorway, Gary stepped over Bucco's lifeless body and started for the stairs when Koto, who was still on his back, reached up and grabbed his ankle.

Gary thought he was knocked out but soon realized that his assailant was still ready to fight. Even so, Gary turned slightly, with his gun still in hand, decided instead to kick Koto in the head, that once again knocked him out.

His ankle released Gary, holstered his gun and walked back downstairs and found the rolling table bar and poured himself a two-finger glass of whiskey.

Sitting down on the deep purple couch, he looked around the massive living room, shook his head and said out loud, "What a waste!"

After what seemed to be a half hour, but was only fifteen minutes, Gary heard the sirens. They were approaching the house at a quick pace.

Gary got up from the couch, placed his finished drink on the bar and walked to the foyer to open the door, just as the door was pushed wide open and there stood Captain O'Keefe, Jack and four other uniformed police officers.

Jack ran through the doorway past everyone else and grabbed Gary and hugged him, kissing him on the cheek. Chuckling, Gary said, "Hey Jack, how are you doing?" Jack smiled back at him and "Better than you, I suppose!"

Meanwhile, Captain O'Keefe directed his men to check on the two criminals upstairs, then turned to Gary and said, "What in the blazing hell happened?"

Gary told O'Keefe that he had been followed to the house and that he figured that they knew another way into it when he went in through the front entry. Then he found them upstairs coming out of the master bedroom and that both thugs had jumped him. After the scuffle, he shot Bucco dead, since he was coming at him with a knife. He almost killed Koto, with the glass table, but then had to kick him in his head to stay down!

Jack said, "Well what matters the most is that you are OK?"

Gary smiled and said, "Time for a steam and a massage, to remedy this morning."

Captain O'Keefe snapped, "On your own dime Marine. Sorry, police policy."

Gary hallway chuckled as Jack, and he walked towards the doors to exit the house.

When the ambulance came to take Koto to the hospital, Captain O'Keefe instructed the police officers who were escorting him to make sure that no one was permitted to see him unless O'Keefe gave his approval.

Koto had lost much blood, and the paramedics didn't know if he would make it through the night informing O'Keefe that they would do what they could.

The coroner's van took Bucco's body away and was instructed to keep it a secret and secure and that no one other than the Captain and immediate people were to know about it.

Back at the precinct, O'Keefe discussed what he knew with Jack and Gary.

The Captain said, "There has been a lot of bloodshed over some stupid contracts where the mob might reap $100,000 or so. Why it seems too little for them to be involved with?"

The Captain then went on with his thoughts. Even an attorney, Alan Glass, got roughed up over this. Every place we turn, there seems to be violence beyond the normal crap to get Donnie to sign the damn contract with Barcelino. We need to put an end to it now!"

Other concerns from O'Keeffe was about Bugsy Siegel.

Bugsy had been traveling back and forth into Mexico, according to Feds and other San Diego agencies. It worried the LAPD since the Mob had lost out on their drug trafficking from Turkey because of the War, it needed a fresh supply to keep the money flowing in their lucrative business. Just south of San Diego in Baja, Bugsy had set his operations up, and it was proving to be just as much as a nuisance as extortion of the entertainment industry.

Furthermore, after moving to Hollywood in 1942, an unknown actress began working with Siegel in his Baja operations. She became his mistress in spite of his marriage.

Lastly, O'Keefe told Jack and Gary that the Feds had arrested one of the Mob's men, Johnny Roselli and several other members on racketeering charges. Even if the Feds were spread thin, they were able to convict several of the Family members, keeping things somewhat under control.

Jack told her Uncle she understood but disagreed with him on the $100,000 limit that the mob would receive by signing Donnie. She told him that having another record company in Chicago's pocket would only add to the millions of dollars that would be made throughout the years to come.

Music is Life…and Death
Chapter 13

In the hospital, Norma was sitting next to Alan, feeding him some soft farina and orange juice when Donnie peaked into the room and said, "Any left for me?"

Alan with his face still bandaged up from the stitches half smiled, as Norma said, "Good Morning Mr. Heaven."

Donnie walked over to the bed and grabbed Alan's hand.

He said, "Man, I am so sorry. I never thought that it would get to this level. I've notified Captain O'Keefe and told him that Joey was putting the squeeze on everyone, but I am not sure how much that will mean since both the Sheriff's Department and the LAPD have some corrupt officers, so we might have to hire some of our own muscle to keep us safe."

Alan looked at Donnie and wanted to say something, but then pointed to the pad of paper and pen sitting on the table by the door.

Donnie understood what Alan meant. After retrieving the items, Alan began to write. When he was done, he gave the pad to Donnie to read.

It said, "You/we have two choices, provided that Bebop approves it as well. One, we all leave town, which is not practicable or two, we go and see Barcelino and work something out. After all, he is a business person, albeit a criminal. Maybe there is a middle ground for us. Perhaps a timetable, along with a percentage that could be achieved. Something other than total ownership."

Donnie scanned the pad again, thinking if what Alan said, could be worked out with Barcelino. So far it seemed that unless he didn't own at least 50%, there was no way to negotiate with him. But Donnie, said to Alan, "I'll try and set up a meeting and will let you know."

In Brentwood, Barcelino was pacing across his very large 800 square foot bedroom. Alongside the floor to ceiling windows a young woman was lying in his bed, dressed in a cream color satin robe who paged nonchalantly through a Life magazine and made funny sounds as she looked at the stars and celebrities on each page, reading aloud the captions.

Staring almost through her, Joey finally told the woman to shut up. She pouted and rolled over onto her back and told Joey "Come back to bed. I need you again!"

Joey was not having any of it and told her, "Get dressed, go home. I have a business to attend to."

With that, the woman left the room and Joey reached for his phone to call Bucco's apartment. There was no answer. Joey then tried Koto's phone number with the same result.

"What the hell," he thought. "Something has gone wrong, and I need to find out what!"

Barcelino took a shower then dressed and called his next in command, Louis De Luca. He was sometimes called "Louie Lucky" because he had escaped prison more times than not, for lack of witnesses in his successful assassinations and extortions.

Louie was laying low since participating in a recent murder in Florida, which was pre-arranged by the Family. Louie, who stayed in the shadows, was a hit-man for hire and on this afternoon, he answered the call from Joey and agreed to meet him at his home at 2 PM.

Across town looking at a chart in the city morgue, the doctor on duty was Dr. Anthony Martino. The police informed him that the body recently brought in was to be interned with the name of John Doe and that no one was to know that it was there.

Not known to Captain O'Keefe, Martino was the nephew of Barcelino and was not used to the police telling him what he could and could not do. Even if it was a city civil service position, the police had no authority over the medical examiner department.

He questioned the police, "What should I do with the body?" "Am I allowed to examine and perform the standard autopsy?"

The sergeant in charge only said "No!"

Curious about who was in storage, Martino opened the compartment door after the cops left, where the suspicious body was and pulled out the tray uncovering the sheet and saw that it was Bucco. He gasped. It was his "godfather."

"What had happened and why was he killed and left here with these directions from the cops?", thought the doctor.

Martino, who was now feeling nervous and shook up, decided he would call his uncle to let him know what had happened to Mickey. Maybe he could shed some light on what happened?

At the Barcelino residence, Randolph the butler, answered the phone and informed Anthony that Mr. Barcelino was not to be disturbed since he was in conference.

Anthony told the butler, "But it's very important Randolph," who then replied, "I can't interrupt him by his direct orders, but I will inform him that you called when he is finished with his conversation."

Anthony then said, "Tell him it's about Mickey."

Randolph replied, "I will."

Music is Life…and Death
Chapter 14

Back at the precinct, Jack was discussing with Gary and her
Uncle what had taken place at Linsky's, and her thoughts
on the mob's involvement.

"Would there be any repercussions from the death of Bucco
and what about Koto," Jack asked?

Captain O'Keefe, replied, "Unfortunately there could be a
problem since some of the cops with the LAPD are paid by
Barcelino. Sometimes we have been able to find out who
they are, but then another one is bought off. It seems to be
never-ending."

"So," Gary chimed in, "This means that Bucco's death will
no doubt be conveyed to Barcelino and we can expect some
sort of reprisal from it?"

"Yep," the Captain replied. "Regrettably, he has eyes and
ears everywhere, so we should be prepared for anything."

Thinking out loud Jack said, "Well, we better get to the
bottom of Linsky's murder before anyone else ends up on
the slab."

Hours later, the Captain called the morgue and asked for
the sheriff on duty and was told by the assistant nurse that
he left and no one replaced him.

The Captain's responded with "Oh! You are telling me that
no other deputy or police officer is on duty there?"

The nurse replied, "That's what I am saying."

Hanging up the phone, O'Keefe turned to Jack and Gary and said, "Geez, it's already begun. Barcelino knows about Bucco. The County Sheriff, Duff, was pulled off the morgue, so no telling who informed Barcelino."

Jack looked at Gary and said, "I am going to visit Mr. Chung again. He might be able to talk to Barcelino before this gets more out of hand than it is already."

Calling Jimmy Woo, Jack told Jimmy that it was urgent to talk to Chung.

Jimmy said he would call her back as soon as it could be arranged.

After hanging up, Gary told Jack that he was going to the hospital to talk to Alan Glass about what the shakedown was all about. Maybe he could tie together Bucco and Koto to Randy, Linsky, Glass, and Heaven.

Jack replied, "Don't forget about Buster. He was also one of the names on the unsigned contract."

Gary nodded and said, "I'll catch up with you later. Call me at the hospital to tell me about the meeting with Chung."

Upon Gary leaving, O'Keefe said, "I am sending one of my own men to the morgue to see if the body is still there. In the meantime, I am going to the hospital myself to check on Koto. I haven't heard anything so I am concerned if we still have him in custody. Do you want to tag along?"

Jack replied, "I think I'll wait till Jimmy calls me back. I want to have that conversation with Chung."

"Suit yourself," the Captain replied, "Be careful out there."

"OK," Jack grinned and looked for a magazine to page through till Jimmy called back.

In Brentwood, Randolph told Barcelino that his nephew had called, but Joey told Randolph that Anthony would have to wait till he completed his meeting with Louie.

In the oak walled drawing room, that looked like it was part of a movie set, Joey spoke to Louie.

"I need for you to go and find Bucco & Koto. I am concerned that neither has contacted me since going to Linsky's house. Whatever the issue is I want you to resolve it quickly and quietly. I do not need any more loose ends. I am tired of these guys not taking care of business. On the other hand, Linsky's death was unavoidable, but it needed to be done because Chicago and Miami demanded it. As far as I know, Dick had stepped over the line, and the Syndicate thought he was a liability. Anyway, I don't need Chicago coming down on us."

Louie told Joey, "No problem, I will take care of it."

After that, Louie left, and Barcelino checked with Randolph if there were any more calls or visitors. Finding out that no one else had called, Joey dialed his nephew at the morgue.

When the call came in, Dr. Martino was pacing around Bucco's body in the oversized lab at the city morgue.

Picking up the phone, he heard the wheezing sound that he knew and started to speak rapidly.

"Uncle, is that you? Something terrible has happened, and I don't understand what to do?"

"Anthony, slow down" the reply came. "What terrible thing my son?"

"Mickey, my godfather, he is dead!"

"What" replied Joey. "How can this be?"

"I don't know Uncle," except that the cops brought his body in and told me to keep him under a John Doe. But they didn't tell me anything about how it happened!"

"Well, now I know why I hadn't heard from him."

Thinking about this Joey paused.

Anthony not hearing anything asked, "What should I do?"

"Nothing," Joey responded. "However, try and find out if Koto is in the hospital and where in case he is still alive. The cops might want to keep his death or if he is alive under wraps as well. Then come to my house."

Anthony told him he would and hung up.

Music is Life...and Death
Chapter 15

Part of the War effort or relief came from "The Hollywood Canteen."

Established in early 1942 by John Garfield and Bette Davis, it was located in an old barn on Cahuenga in Los Angles that was converted to allow members of the armed forces to visit, dance and hang out with many stars and entertainment industry people. With the help from talent agencies and others, the Canteen could handle up to 2000 uniform guys every night except Sundays.

It was a "no booze" location, but flasks of all types appeared on the ledges and sometimes broken on the floor after each night.

To many a lonely guy or girl, it was a place where a rendezvous or "hook-up" occurred, in spite of "a no-romance" policy existed.

Dick Linsky and Alice Ray were frequent participants in the Canteen and gave money and time to make sure it was a success.

Mistakenly some of Dick's money came from the mob (who were his investors), as part of his travels, back and forth the Atlantic, as a courier. He was paid for small parcels not inspected that he either carried to France, Italy, Germany or back from these locations. Usually, he could carry them on the plane, but occasionally it was part of his baggage, stored in the belly of the plane, which went undetected.

The last parcel that Dick was carrying to Italy gave specific details for an invasion from the Allies, stolen from the D.C. War room by Sergeant Guerino (Nino) Martino, the youngest brother of Dr. Anthony Martino.

The Sergeant, who was one of the many assistants for General Harris, was not vetted beyond the normal secret investigation by the FBI, because the thinking was that military members already had a clearance.

Dick had handed the large envelope to the "skycap" to hold, at the Burbank Airport. The Los Angeles Airport had opened in 1930 but was known as Mines Field, until 1940 when the name changed. But the major flights hadn't moved to that location.

As the skycap was standing there, Dick was getting his bags from the trunk of Alice's car. All of a sudden, a gust of wind blew the envelope out of the sky cap's his hands ripping the corner of the envelope in such a way that it tore the closure, and the paper and diagrams inside spewed out onto the ground.

The skycap, Alice, and Dick were utterly surprised and looked at each and then started picking up all the papers apologizing to each other as they stacked them up into each other's hands. Alice didn't say anything to Dick but was stunned by what she thought she saw.

After they were able to collect all the papers, Dick told the skycap to please get the rest of his bags as he placed all the papers together and stuffed them into his briefcase.

Dick was not sure what was on these many sheets of paper but was now shaking at the thought of what he might be carrying, based on what he thought he saw.

Dick had always made it a point not to question anyone from his "investors" what he might be carrying back and forth. He always felt that he was above this sort of hide and seek game. So, after saying goodbye to Alice, he walked into the terminal to his gate and waited for his plane.

Alice stood there for a few minutes wanting to say something to him but was afraid to raise any suspicion about what he had in his hands. Not wanting to place Dick in any sort of jeopardy, she got back in her car and drove off.

Checking his bags and sitting down in the waiting area, Dick figured he would place the papers back in order, so he opened his case and started looking through each page for a page number. Though he found them, his eyes strayed to the content and headings and realized that he was looking at something much bigger and important then what he could surmise, and much more secretive than anything he should know.

He was in awe of the details of the invasion, how many, when, hours it would take, supplies and the ships that would carry the troops and equipment. He felt himself beginning to sweat and took off his jacket. Then he heard, "Flight 22 to New York, Gate 6, now boarding.

With that, he stuffed the papers back in his case, grabbed his coat and walked up to the flight attendant to hand her his ticket.

Looking up from the counter, the attendant smiling at Dick, who was now perspiring, said, "Mr. Linsky, are you alright?"

Dick, half smiled and replied, "might have been something I ate this morning, but I am fine."

With that, Dick walked down to the runway and then to the plane awaiting outside. Once inside the cabin, Dick sat alone in first class, where he asked the stewardess for a glass of water.

He sat back and closed his eyes and waited for the plane to take off. After taxiing down the runway, the PAN AM flight was on its way to New York.

There, Dick would take three more flights to get to Rome. It was a very long trip.

A short nap later, Dick woke up to some turbulence, that the Captain announced that they would be out of it shortly. Dick looked out the window and then reached into his case and took out all the papers again.

He decided to not look at what was on the papers but to sort them correctly, and after about 10 minutes, he was able to place them in the exact sequence. With an empty folder that he had in his case, he placed the papers inside and snapped the closure on the folder then placed it on the seat next to him.

Dozing off again, Dick slept restlessly through the clouds to Dallas. Arriving at Love Field, Dick rushed to a nearby phone and called Alice to make sure that she was fine and to see if anyone was looking for him.

Alice told him that Mickey Bucco had stopped by, but that was all.

Dick told her, "Oh, Ok, no problem, I am fine, and I'll call you from my next stop," and hung up.

His next flight was not scheduled for another hour, so he walked the length of the terminal to get some exercise, passing by a few makeshift tented commercial shops, that sold cosmetics and clothing items. The permanent stores were still in the throes of being built.

Walking back through the gate to his plane, Dick thought that a looking Italian gentleman was following him. He didn't remember the man on the plane but saw him walking along the same pathway in the terminal, where Dick was walking.

Finally, back on the plane and after sitting down, the Italian looking man entering the plane observed Dick, and walked past him and went into the economy section of the plane.

Dick felt a bit uneasy, and once again some perspiration appeared on his forehead as the same stewardess approached Dick and asked him again if there was anything, she could do for him.

Dick smiled and said, "No Thank You, really, I am fine."

About halfway into the flight as Dick was about to nap when the Italian man, stood alongside his seat and startled him.

Dick tried to squeeze further back into his seat, as he gained his wits about him.

The Italian looking man sensing the uneasiness spoke first. "Mr. Linsky, I am sorry to awaken you, but I wanted you to know who I was and why I am on the plane with you."

Dick, realizing that the man couldn't do any harm to him, acknowledged his intruder with a half-hearted grin.

The man began to speak again. "Mr. Linsky, my name is Louie De Luca, I am a friend of Mr. Bucco's, and he wanted to make sure you made your trip safely and securely. So, I am here as your bodyguard till you deliver your package. I hope you understand our concerns for whatever your package contains and that it does not stray into the wrong hands?"

Dick, guardedly grinned back, then looked in his lap, while the man walked back to his seat where he began to read his magazine.

Without any further interaction for the next four hours, after landing, Louie walked past Dick as he departed the plane and just smiled at him.

Dick collected his bag and coat then proceeded out of the plane by himself, feeling a bit edgy that someone was overshadowing him on this trip. No one had ever done so in the past. Why was this trip more important than the rest? It must be the papers he had in his briefcase he surmised.

Secretive and vital documents for someone that Dick neither wanted to know or find out what it was for caused Dick to be more nervous than ever before.

Finding a phone booth, Dick attempted to call Alice but found himself speaking with her butler, who informed him that she was at the "Canteen" working on the night's festivities.

Cussing under his breath, he hung up the phone and walked to a small diner in the waiting lounge of the New York Municipal Airport for his flight to Rome.

An hour and a half later he was boarding the PAN AM flight for Italy. After settling in, the stewardess asked Dick if he wanted anything to drink, which he declined stating that he just wanted to read and nap.

Two seats behind Dick in the economy section sat another gentleman from the Outfit, Mr. Greenstein. His sole job was to monitor Dick on his trip to Rome and make sure that no one was following him and that he delivered his package.

Though Dick was a movie star, his position was enhanced by his association with The Outfit and their major influence over the movie studios.

It so happened that Frank Nitti and other organized members were accused of extortion of MGM, Paramount and the like. Threats of shutting down the unions that built the sets with all the electricians, woodworkers and laborers, caused the studios to pay large sums to make sure business was normal in Hollywood.

More than once, one of the Outfit "lieutenants" would visit a set where Dick was on to make sure that he was receiving everything he needed and if Dick said "no," the head of the studio would be visited by someone with absurd pressure, to make sure that Dick had no issues.

During the flight in first class to Rome, Dick found himself engaged in a lively conversation with an Italian young man, by the name of Giuseppe Bianco, who was from a small town in the Tuscany area – Lucca.

Giuseppe was a baker who inherited his father's shop, who recently had passed away. In taking over the bakery, he had to go to New York to get the recipes from his uncle Gino, his father's brother.

It would seem that Giuseppe's dad never wrote anything down to follow. So, he had to sit with his uncle and carefully write down everything to make sure that he didn't lose any business after re-opening the shop, in the small town.

Being invited to his shop, Dick assured Giuseppe that he would stop in on his way from his travels before returning to the States. And as they left the plane, Giuseppe kissed Dick on the right cheek.

Mr. Greenstein was standing away from the two gentlemen but watched the conversation without expression and followed Dick to baggage. After Dick had retrieved his belongings, he went out to find a taxi to his hotel.

Stepping into the next waiting taxi, Mr. Greenstein told the driver to follow the cab in front of him.

After twenty minutes, they both had reached the area closest to the World Exposition area that never took place. Originally built by Mussolini and his Fascist party, with references to the ancient Imperial Rome, all the buildings were constructed and never used.

The hotel past this area on the other side of the Basilica of Peter was the Palazzo Cardinal Cesi.

After checking in and arranging his clothes, Dick decided to take a nap before supper. However, just as he was laying his clothes out on the bed, there was a knock on his door.

Opening the door, Mr. Greenstein stood there, introduced himself and asked if he could come in.

Dick was surprised but let him in after finding out that he was from the Chicago Syndicate.

Mr. Greenstein got right down to business by asking Dick, "Do you still have the package?"

Dick, pointed to the dresser and said, "Yes."

Mr. Greenstein then said, "Fine, please hand it over to me, and I will take it from here."

Dick acting surprised, said, "I thought I was supposed to deliver this myself?"

Mr. Greenstein, replied, "Change of plans; that's why I am here."

Dick responded, "Ok, then what should I do, wait for a response?"

Mr. Greenstein replied, "Yes, please. I will come back in a few days with your return package."

Dick, thinking that everything was Ok, said, "Alright then, a few days."

But Mr. Greenstein said, "You mustn't go to Lucca to see Giuseppe!"

Dick looked at Mr. Greenstein and said, "How do you know about him?"

Greenstein, replied, "I was on the plane with you. It's protocol you know?"

Dick didn't know that he was followed all the way and wasn't trusted to do his part.

Greenstein then said, "Safety Mr. Linsky is our most important job. No one is to know where you are and what you do, understand?"

Dick nodded his head as Greenstein left the room.

Walking to the window, he looked out at the afternoon passersby on the street. Dick was amazed that he was not trusted after all this time, but then it must have to do with the documents he carried.

Deciding he would have to wait for Greenstein's return, Dick went to bed, hoping to sleep the whole night.

After a few days of waiting for Greenstein and not hearing anything, Dick decided to take a trip to Lucca to see Giuseppe. After all, even though he was advised not to do this, he was bored hanging around all day with nothing to do.

Checking with the front desk, he was able to hire a car for the trip to see Giuseppe.

It was nearly 4 PM when the driver, Pietro Assisi told Dick that it was about a 5 or 6, hour drive and would cost about 200,000 lire.

Dick agreed and informed the hotel that he would be away for two days and then return.

Dick was unaware that Mr. Greenstein had gone to the hotel around 5 PM and found out that Dick had left, despite his directions to stay there.

Greenstein went back to his room and made a call for instructions from Chicago and now waited for Dick to return.

At 11:15 PM, Pietro arrived at the address in Lucca that Dick had given him. The bakery was closed, but the lights were on, and Giuseppe was cleaning tables and talking to someone in the back when Dick knocked on the window.

Smiling, Giuseppe opened the door to greet Dick. "How is my American friend from New York?"

Dick said, "Tired, but happy to see you."

They hugged and kissed each other's cheek, smiled at one another and Giuseppe said, "Sit, please."

Dick did as he was told, and Giuseppe went around the counter to pour some coffee.

He asked, Dick, "Do you have someplace to stay tonight?"

Dick, replied, "No, I hadn't even thought about that!"

The young man smiled and said, "Dick, you stay with us tonight, me and Gina, my sister. It will be Okay, right Gina?", calling out to her, who was in the back of the store.

Answering the question Gina replied, "Sure whatever you say, brother."

Two days later, Dick returned to his hotel in Rome. There he found a note from Mr. Greenstein stating that he would meet him at the airport the next morning.

Dick was wondering how Greenstein knew that he was back, but the thought came and went as he began packing for his trip back to the States.

Other than Mr. Greenstein giving a new package for Dick to carry back to the States, he was not very pleasant and not on the plane. Nor was there anyone else that followed Dick home, as he called Alice from each stop he made.

After returning to the Burbank Airport, there was the driver from Barcelino holding a sign up high for Dick. Taking Dick outside to the car, he returned to pick up Dick's bags and dropped Dick off at his house.

The driver had taken the package, and so Dick thought everything was okay and went about his business of settling back into his home life.

At the prescient in Hollywood, sitting in a taped up broken chair, Donnie was speaking with Capt. O'Keefe about Dick, Alan, along with his own involvement with Joey Barcelino and the contract that had seemed to have caused all these problems and death.

O'Keefe, listening to his friend was not happy nor was he willing to accept "I don't know" from Donnie as they talked about everyone that seemed to be involved.

The Captain said to Donnie, "So you are telling me that you do not know why Dick was killed?"

Donnie replied, "Listen, Mike, it is true that Dick and I were occasional lovers, but we also led different lives, had different friends, and quite frankly other than a romp occasionally we rarely saw each other. Whatever his association with Barcelino or anyone else, if any, was his business. It did not include me, nor I with him."

O'Keefe, said, "Well maybe it was independent of you since the Mob has had its hands into every entertainment business sector for years, I have no reason not to think that Dick was also part of it somehow and they didn't need him any longer."

The Captain went on to say that he would assign a police officer to shadow Donnie until they found out who, what and where, but in the meantime, he needed to stay in touch and not leave town.

Music Is Life…and Death
Chapter 16

By the time Jimmy called, Jack had been able to piece
together something of Dick and Donnie's relationship with
Barcelino. They were different, but both had a purpose.
Besides muscling the movie studios, and the unions, Joey
used Dick as the go between the Mob and someone in Italy,
but what and why?

On the other hand, Donnie was a connection between the
recording and movie studios and the Mob. Without either
of these two men, the Mob would have had to infiltrate the
entertainment industry with someone else.

Because each man seemed to serve a purpose, it was
imperative to keep their connection separately, to make
sure that the Mob received their fair share of the profits in
this worldwide economy, especially during wartime.

But why murder Randy and Dick? Egos or fear, Jack
thought. Why did any of this matter in the big picture? It
was still a puzzle.

Jimmy informed Jack that Mr. Chung could meet with her
that afternoon at 3 PM to discuss what he had found out.

Since it was almost 12:30, Jack drove over to the
Hollywood Canteen first to see if Alice was still there and
if she could shed any more information on why Dick was
murdered?

As she drove from the police station on La Brea to the
Canteen, she stopped at Sunset Boulevard and noticed that
there was a black Chevrolet behind her with two men
inside. Making a mental note, she turned right and

continued to drive slowly towards Cahuenga Blvd, where the Canteen was located.

At the stop light, she turned right and looked for a parking spot. Finding it directly across the street from the Canteen, she pulled in just in time to see the "Chevy" drive slowly pass her car.

Jack made sure that she wrote down the license number (VHU 451), as the car sped away on Cahuenga. Peering deep in the car she saw two guys staring back at her. Both Italian looking, she was sure of it.

In her mind, she wondered who they worked for but already knew the answer, that Joey was behind it.

Crossing the street, Jack saw that there was a line of Servicemen standing alongside the barn that extended down the block to Fountain.

Jack thought, "How do I get in," as she stared at the building looking for an entrance.

Many of the "boys" were now smiling and whistling as she walked past them around the side looking for a door. Finally finding what she was looking for, the sign read "Volunteer Help Entrance."

Walking through the doorway, Jack was greeted by the actress Alice Fay, according to her name tag along with an unfamiliar actress, that she had never seen her before.

Jack said, "Alice, my name is Jacqueline Riley, a private detective helping the LAPD. Do you have a moment to speak to me about Dick Linsky?"

Alice looked surprised, but said, "Ah, yes, Trixie can you mind the entrance. I know that Ms. Davis and Mr. Rains will be showing up any minute. They are coming from the set, "Now, Voyager." Please let me know when they arrive. Thanks."

Taking Jack's left arm, Alice led her to a back office, after dodging several Army and Navy guys using the restrooms.

Shutting the door, Alice asked, "What can I do for you or say that I haven't already told the police?"

Jack replied, "There is one person at the center of this murder which may be at the center of another unsolved murder. We are trying to tie it together, so we can make the appropriate arrests and lock these guys up for good. So, I am hoping that you can tell me more about Dick and his travels, etc., to help me find the connection."

Alice sat there for a minute and then said, "Dick would normally tell me what and where he was when he traveled. Though he would never say who he was working for or what he was doing."

"Strangely," Alice continued, "On the last trip he stopped and called me a bunch of times, going to Europe. Once in Dallas, then in New York and then when he was in a town in Italy called Lucca. He always sounded like he was trying to be secretive, telling me where he was and who he was with. In Dallas, it was an Italian man, but I never got his name. In New York, to Italy, it was Giuseppe Bianco and Mr. Greenstein. In Lucca, it was Giuseppe."

"Had you ever met either of these men before," asked Jack.

"No," said Alice. "Never heard of any of them, nor did I want to pry into Dick's business. On his return, he never made mention of anyone else, so I assumed he was alone?"

Jack tried something different then. "How about the day Dick left. Did you drop him off at the airport?"

"Yes," said Alice. "And you know what, there was something that occurred that day, that was very strange. While Dick was moving his luggage from the trunk of the car to the baggage cart, a gust of wind blew the envelope out of the skycap's hands onto the curb. On the ground were papers and maps that read 'Top Secret.' Helping Dick and the skycap pick these up, I never said a word to Dick about what they looked like to me. But I knew, and Dick looked at me with puppy dog eyes that said, "Please do not ask me what they are..."

"Maps and top secret, wow that's it," said Jack.

Alice said, "What?"

"Sure, the Mob has been helping the Navy, and the war efforts, but maybe this time they were going in the opposite direction and playing both sides. More than likely Dick was a courier who moved these documents back and forth without anyone asking him about them. He probably never knew that these were secret plans regarding the Allies."

Alice looked at Jack dumbfounded, and Jack just stared through her thinking of what to do next.

After a few silent moments, Jack told Alice that she would surely like to come back to the Canteen on a happier note when Alice said that she was welcome anytime as they shook hands.

Music Is Life…and Death
Chapter 17

By the time that Louie called Joey that the Linsky's house
was swarming with cops, Joey told him the news about
Bucco and told Louie to get to the Good Samaritan
Hospital to check on Koto, where the police had taken him.

Anthony, Joey's nephew, had already called the County
Sheriff and told him that Koto needed to be moved before
the LAPD cops arrived.

When the two uniformed cops came to relieve the original
cops standing guard over Koto, they were informed that the
County Sheriff and his officers took over the watch.

Wanting to confirm this, the officers went upstairs to room
212, to find it empty and no Sheriff Deputies on duty.

Irritated that the County Sheriff would interfere with their
hostage, the police walked to the nurse's station on the
floor and asked what time Koto had been released?

Meeting the officers on the second floor, Captain O'Keefe
heard what they were asking the nurse and started yelling.

He said, "Young lady, who released Mr. Koto?

Seeing how upset he was, the nurse replied that the head
nurse, Mrs. Hatch had received a phone call and whoever
was on the phone had enough authority to release Koto to
Sheriff Duff.

Fuming with this turn of events, O'Keefe demanded to
speak to the head nurse.

Ten minutes later, Mrs. Hatch came rushing towards O'Keefe and said, "Captain, I am very sorry for the wait. I was assisting one of the doctors in the emergency. I understand that you wanted to know who told me to release Mr. Koto. It was a call from Dr. Martino, at the city morgue, stating that the police had given their okay to release him to the Sheriff."

O'Keefe, knowing darn well that it hadn't come from him or his department said, "I understand. How would you know that we hadn't okayed this? So, thank you for your time and trouble."

Outside in the patrol car, O'Keefe called Sergeant O'Shay and relayed the status of their prisoner. It was now a tug of war between the city cops and the county cops. Corruption on both sides did not help in the arrest and incarceration of many criminals. O'Keefe knew that he would need Jack and Gary to help solve this once and for all.

Driving out of LA city proper into the county, Sheriff Duff spoke to Koto who was sitting in the back of the car. The doctors had patched him up as best as they could before releasing him.

Sheriff Duff told Koto that he needed to get out of town, maybe go to Vegas or Chicago where he could be protected.

Koto agreed and said, "I will when Joey tells me to go!"

Dropping Koto off at Barcelino's house in Brentwood, Sheriff Duff sped off in the direction of his office in downtown on Temple St, just south of Chinatown.

Oblivious to Duff, he was being followed by Louie Lucky.

After Duff got to his office, Louie called Joey, to tell him that the Sheriff was the one that sprang Koto free. Joey told him that he knew because Koto just recapped what had happened at Linsky's house.

Louie then asked Joey "What was to be done with the Sheriff, if anything."

Joey told him "Nothing, for now, we may need him one more time before this is over. Come back here; I have a job for you."

Music Is Life...and Death
Chapter 18

At the Metro Hospital, Gary was speaking with Alan Glass about the contract, Donnie and Barcelino. Alan, the attorney that he was, kept stating that Joey wanted to control everything and that Donnie wanted to be free of the Mob, which appeared was not going to happen. Regarding Dick Linsky, he knew very little of his entanglements with Joey or anyone else.

Gary thanked him for his time and went to the nurse station to use the phone. First, he called O'Keefe and found out from O'Shay that Koto was free and that the Captain hadn't returned yet but that they had placed an "all-points bulletin" out on Koto.

Gary told O'Shay that he was still at the Metro and that if the Captain or Jack were looking for him to contact him there.

Visiting with Mr. Chung, Jack asked him again about the relationship between the Barcelino organization and Chung.

He was surprised that she would ask him repeatedly and confirmed that he knew nothing of what Joey was up to, nor anything about the Linsky murder. However, Chung told Jack that Sheriff Duff had gotten Koto released from the hospital and to his knowledge Koto was taken to Joey's home.

Jack didn't want to know how he found this out but thanked him for this information.

"Furthermore," Chung said, "Joey had called me to discuss the incident in Chinatown, stating that it was nothing personal, but that he was looking for some documents that belonged to him and that Randy had stolen them from him and unfortunately they had found him with May."

Joey also told Chung that he would pay for any damages incurred, though it appeared that it was only lip service, according to Chung.

Barcelino wanted to strut his presence and power in Los Angles. However, Mr. Chung told Joey that he knew nothing about the documents and that May was now in his control, and if he learned of anything else from her that he would call Joey.

Joey sensed the coldness on the phone from Chung, then said to him, "Thank you, I would appreciate the respect and continued business that we share" and then hung up the phone.

Chung went on to tell Jack that he believed that Joey knew that he was lying, but there wasn't anything Joey could do unless he wanted to go to war with Chinatown.

Back at the hospital, Gary took a seat in the waiting area, waiting for Jack to call to see what their next move would be.

Waiting was not a productive time for Gary, but he started reading an article from the April 13th issue of "Life" magazine on the Army Supply Chief, Major General Marshall when the phone rang, and the nurse on duty called out Gary's name.

"Here," he said after the nurse repeated it several times.

"Jack, what's the news on your end?"

She told Gary that loose ends were everywhere and there seemed to be no end in sight of piecing it together.

Once again, they agreed to meet up at the Precinct to discuss what they all had learned and where they needed to focus their energies and resources.

Music Is Life…and Death
Chapter 19

O'Keefe, Riley, and Jackson sat in a large open space in the police station on La Brea.

The Captain then quizzed the police officers if any of them had heard anything new involving the Dick Linsky or Randy Winter murders. There was some speculation but no real leads as they spoke to each officer.

Jack proposed that they might want to start looking elsewhere and gave her reasons, to begin with, ASA, the talent agency, owned primarily by Irving Friedman, another somewhat recluse doctor.

The company had started in Cleveland and had a long list of clients and associates from the old days up to the present that included gangsters and actors alike. Friedman also fashioned his business after the fairly famous eye doctor, Jules Stein of MCA fame. It seemed that the two of them owned a lot of "turf" that included actors, singers, and other entertainment businesses.

As stories go, there is one told of an associate at an agency, who had threatened to cut of Tommy Dorsey's private parts for trying to get out of his contract.

Jack, who seemed to be thinking out loud, felt that stirring up the pot with ASA might shake things up and provide some additional leads into their current case, told her Uncle and Gary where she was going.

On the other hand, Gary had mentioned that since Dick traveled so much, there might be something that the Feds or the military might know and that he would press a few of his old cronies to see what he could learn.

The Captain said "Great, but try and keep it under wraps, as we do our due diligence from the legal side and the Sheriff's ears."

When Jack arrived at the ASA offices at 360 North Crescent Dr in Beverly Hills, she was in awe. The building was a sprawling English Georgian design with a parking garage, gardens with fountains and statuary.

Originally built by Paul. R Williams, he had been coined as "the architect of the stars."

It was only appropriate, for this man and his company that came from a basement home in Ohio that he would want something so grand to entice its clients to stay. It signaled to the world, "That it was all about money."

Walking into the foyer and reception area, Jack handed the girl behind the counter her card and asked if she could speak with the senior attorney for the company.

She explained that as a private investigator, she was part of the LAPD force examining the murder of Dick Linsky.

The girl said, "no problem" and rang an office, as Jack sat down in the waiting area.

About fifteen minutes passed when an older gentleman, about 60 years of age approached Jack and said, "I'm sorry for the wait, Ms. Riley, I'm Sheldon Glasser, Senior Attorney for ASA. I understand you are assisting the Los Angeles Police in solving the Dick Linsky murder?"

Jack stood up and was surprised that she was about five inches taller than Mr. Glasser, but responded with "Yes, I work with them periodically on unsolved cases."
Mr. Glasser then said, "Please, if you don't mind follow me to our conference room."

When entering the room, Jack found that there were two other men seated. Neither man spoke yet was dressed in the same type of business suits as Mr. Glasser.

The Senior Attorney, only referred to them as "associates" during the entire hour that she was there. The most information she was able to find out was that Dick was one of their top clients at ASA. He had been a huge success for ASA and that it would be hard to replace him at the studios at this point.

Glasser went on to say that they had no information on who would have wanted him dead since it appeared that he had no enemies.

Leaving ASA, Jack walked passed Betty Grable, who looked at Jack as if to say, "Hey don't I know you?"

Jack had seen her at the Hollywood Canteen recently handing out food in the chow line and just smiled back as she continued to walk past the famous star.

Gary had to drive thirty-one-miles to the 40th Infantry Division Headquarters, located in Los Alamitos, California. This was where General Harris and his staff usually were located, if not in D.C.

Gary knew a few Marines who guarded the General, along with some of his old Army buddies. So, after getting approval to get on the base, he drove over to the main building where he walked in to meet up with his buds.

After the initial welcome, Gary got down to business asking about the General and his Staff. He jotted the names down as the guys reflected all the members and where they currently were, either on the base or in D.C.

Finding out what he could, it appeared to add something to the mystery of Dick's other life, though it was kept very private and secret. As a matter of fact, as Gary learned, the military was just about ready to arrest Dick on Treason, after finding out that Sergeant Martino had stolen secret documents from the General's office in D.C. The Sergeant was now in the brig on treason charges, and so the military was now searching for Dick.

Gary was stunned by this information and couldn't wait to report this. However, he relayed the unfortunate death of Linsky to his military counterparts, which only closed part of the case against Nino Martino.

By the time Gary, Jack, and O'Keefe got down with their independent investigations, they found themselves back at the house on Hortense going over their notes.

As Gary went through his crumpled papers, the name Martino popped out loud and clear to O'Keefe, as he asked Gary again, "Did you say, Martino?"

Gary said, "Yes, Sergeant Guerino Martino."

"Well there's one connection," said O'Keefe, as both Jack and Gary looked up from what they were reading.

"How's that?" asked her Uncle.

"Well, it just so happens that Dr. Martino's younger brother is named the same. And Martino is the Medical Examiner who was on duty and gave Kim Koto to Sheriff Duff. Who by the way is on the Syndicate's payroll? So, the bodies keep piling up, and the Mob's influence and control seem to be everywhere.

Jack then said, "Wow, at least you got somewhere with your visit, I struck out. Other than controlling the actors and who knows who, ASA does not have any real connection to Dick and his travels to Europe and back. However, the attorney did tell me that Dick used to meet with Mickey Bucco, at the office, which I found strange unless ASA and the Mob are connected?"

O'Keefe chimed in with, "Perhaps Dick had used up his welcome with the Mob, and that's why they took him out since Koto was the trigger man."

Jack said, "Agreed! Either he knew too much, or found out something that he wasn't supposed to, just like Randy Winter."

"Well guys," as Gary began to tell his revelation about Dick's travels from the military.

By the time he completed his story, both the Captain and Jack were shaking their head, since they now knew why he was murdered and by whom.

Music Is Life…and Death
Chapter 20

Since Jack had some apprehension about Chung in finding Koto, after the meeting with Mr. Chung, he had instructed his number one son and bodyguard, Wang Chu, to find Koto and interrogate him till he repeated what he knew.

Wang did as he was instructed and had two men placed at Barcelino's house if Koto showed up. It wasn't but a couple of days when Sheriff Duff dropped Koto off and one of the two men who had been staking out the house drove to get Wang.

When the man arrived in Chinatown at the Red Dragon, Wang told Chung then climbed into the car and sped off to Brentwood.

It took no more than fourteen minutes to get to Barcelino's house, and Wang hoped that nothing had changed since being informed.

When the Black Packard arrived, Wang got out of the car and confirmed with his man that Koto was still in the house.

Towards nightfall, after Louie returned, Joey discussed with Koto that he needed to go to Vegas, to hide out till things blew over in town. Joey told Koto that he would work it out with the cops so that Koto could come back.

After he was instructed to gather his belongings, Louie walked Koto outside to the waiting Chrysler limousine. It was nearly 9 PM.

Wang was told by Chung to follow Koto and got back into his car along with his men and waited for the limo to drive pass the Packard.

In the parlor, before leaving, Joey reminded Koto to stay out of sight and that he would be contacted once things calmed down.

Joey told Koto that Abe Goldblum, who worked with Seigel, would be his contact in Vegas. Then Joey gave Louie his final orders.

As the limo passed the Packard, Wang told his driver to stay at least two car lengths behind, to not raise any suspicion.

Driving through Brentwood, the limo came to the dirt road that was in the process of being paved. This lead from Santa Monica to the Interstate 405 highway. This main highway would deliver them to the US 91 road that ultimately ended in Vegas.

Traveling this way would take about 6 hours to drive the entire distance. After leaving San Bernardino, there was nothing much else except for some very small gasoline stations, restaurants, and hotels, that dotted the two or three-lane blacktop.

About 2:30 in the morning, having driven almost 5 hours or so, Louie turned the limo lights out and pulled off into a dirt road where a sign read, "No Trespassers." It was just a short distance from the town of Jean.

Taking out his gun from its holster Louie placed it on his lap in the dark, as he continued to drive slowly.

Half a mile down the road, Koto who was asleep, woke up and asked Louie, "Where are we and what are we doing?"

Louie without warning stopped the car, lifted the gun in his left hand, turned slightly to face Koto and shot him directly in his forehead. The sound in the vehicle was so loud that Louie lost his hearing for almost an hour.

Koto slumped in the seat with his head against the passenger window, where a small splatter of blood trickled down the glass onto the door.

Louie got out of the car and walked around to the passenger door and let Koto's dead body roll out of the car. Louie proceeded to wipe the car door and window with a towel that he had brought with him and then threw the towel next to Koto's body on the ground.

Stepping back into the Chrysler, Louie's hearing was beginning to return, and he could hear a single car coming down the highway from his open window. He was struggling to air out the smell of death.

Turning the car around, Louie headed towards the highway, turning East towards Jean where he found a motel to spend the night.

The Packard which had been following the limo never saw the dirt road as it drove by at 60 miles an hour towards Vegas.

As the Packard arrived in Sloan, Wang told the driver to stop, as there were no cars in front of them. Pausing to think where they might have lost the limo without spotting it, Wang said, "Turn the car around, we have to find where they turned off!"

Creeping along the highway from Sloan for several miles the men in the Packard were looking at both sides of the road for any signs when on the left they spotted a turn off with the words, "No Trespassing." It was across the road, and Wang told the driver to pull into the road but go slow.

Like a police car, the Packard had a spotlight on the driver side. So as the driver moved the light back and forth across the road, he barely held his foot on the gas pedal.

As the car crept along the dirt road with rocks and pebbles, it seemed like it took forever until they spotted a lifeless body lying alongside the path.

Stopping the driver kept the spotlight on the body as Wang walked up to it. Stooping down, he placed his two right fingers across Koto's neck and felt no pulse.

"Yep," he thought, "He's dead, but shot by whom?"

Wrapping his body in a blanket, they placed him in the trunk to take back to the LAPD, in case they could use it to apprehend whoever shot him. It might also come in handy for Mr. Chung to use against Barcelino, Wang thought.

Driving back out onto the highway and tired from their travels, Wang opted to have them drive to Jean to find a place to stay for the night. Unbeknownst to Wang, they ended up at the same motel as Louie and in fact in the next room.

Strangely, maybe because they were all so tired, no one noticed the limo parked in the back of the motel. Later the following morning both cars left without incident and without knowing they had stayed there at the same hotel for the night.

Music Is Life…and Death
Chapter 21

When Jack woke up in the morning, she didn't think that she'd still be learning how the film and entertainment industry really worked.

Working for the Navy and its affair with the Mafia was something else. But now with the Mob, Chinatown, along with the Entertainment industry in bed together she thought, "Who is not connected to organized crime since there are politicians, law enforcement and the everyday joes attached at the hip in this wacky business."

O'Keefe, Gary and Jack agreed to bring Donnie and his partners into the station to see if they could wrap up the case and set about to locate them.

Except for Alan, who was still in the hospital, O'Keefe ordered a warrant for Donnie and Bebop, to keep them safe.

When the cops knocked on Donnie's door, he was quite surprised, since he had been entertaining a new lover and was very upset at the disturbance but got dressed after sending the young man away and accompanied the police gladly.

Bebop, on the other hand, was at his store and just smiled and told the assistant manager to take over till he returned.

Donnie was the first to arrive and as he reached the Captain's office and tried to be funny but came off the wrong way.

"What the hell is this all about, being brought down to the station like a criminal, I didn't do anything, so why am I here?"

O'Keefe looked at the two officers who had brought Donnie in and waved them off to thank them and then tried to calm down the Hollywood star.

"Donnie, you are not under arrest, but rather protected for the moment as we are trying to solve these two murders along with your situation and your associates."

Donnie stopped pouting and said, "Ok, I am sorry for acting like this. I am trying to meander through this mess myself and come out the back end successful and of course alive."

Gary chimed in with, "Donnie murder is a serious offense, and there have been several committed by Barcelino and his people, so we are looking to stop him and throw him in jail for a very long, long time. You do understand this, right?"

Smiling, Donnie looked around the room and nodded his head.

Jack was next to speak and told Donnie that Koto who murdered Dick had also been killed.

She went on to tell him that no one knew for sure who did it or if it was on Barcelino's orders, but more than likely he didn't want Koto talking to the police about anything.

Donnie was somewhat shocked but knew that this would have been something that Barcelino would do to protect his self and the organization.

Jack continued with what they knew. "Through a series of contacts on my side, we've learned that Chicago has been nervous about Barcelino and instructed Miami to step in and try and smooth things out to quiet down the possible national attention to the mob's fingers in the entertainment business. And though Barcelino did not know this, his days might be numbered if he could not on his own terms take care of the situation."

This time Donnie seemed to be moved by what Jack just said.

O'Keefe smiled and said, "There is a war of attrition here between the Barcelino and Dragna Families to control much of Southern California and Nevada. According to our sources, the Five Families have established a Commission to sort out the issues and to establish only one Family in this area. My concern is that it might turn into a bloodbath before it's over."

Donnie replied, "This can't be about Dick or me? We are minor players within the powerful Mob. They do have their hands in almost everything from the trade unions, corporations, law enforcement, and the government. I don't see where we are part of this entanglement?"

"Donnie," replied O'Keefe, "You are a part of it because it is all about money and control. Dick was part of that as well, who worked with Chicago and Miami and fell out of favor with The Family and paid the ultimate price."

O'Keefe continued, "When Meyer lost his casino business in New York, he went elsewhere. When the studios yelled foul play to the Feds, the Navy hired the Mob to help control the harbors. It's complicated at best but comes down to who is in control of the movies and music along with paying their share back to the Commission and Families."

"Okay," Donnie spoke up. "What should I do at this point?"

O'Keefe looked at Donnie and then to Jack and Gary and said, "You are going to be our guest for a few days while we sort this out and hopefully arrest Barcelino. We will keep you at a safe house with police monitoring it 24/7. Jack and Gary will also be on hand at times. Is that alright? It's the best we know how to do to keep you alive until Joey is behind bars."

Donnie looked at his hands and turned over his palms then once again at the back of his hands and replied, "Okay."

Music Is Life…and Death
Chapter 22

Initially, it was decided that Jack and Gary would drive
Donnie to the "safe house" in an unmarked police car with
two officers assigned for the first twenty-four hours.

The house was off of Montlake Drive that weaved its way
parallel between Griffith Park and Lake Hollywood.

Set amongst the forestry area, you could only get to it if
you knew where you were going since the roads were dirt
that seemed to lead to nowhere, with no signs marking off a
street or address.

Since the start of the War, several of the old buildings were
used as Japanese mini-internment sites before the people
were transported to other processing centers throughout the
States.

From the safe house, it was quite a beautiful location where
you could see the Hollywoodland sign and Lake
Hollywood.

Following the cop car, Jack and Gary made mental and
written notes regarding the road and how to get to the
house in case they had to drive out there alone.

The major issue would be at night. They would have to
keep an eye on the mileage gauge to make sure they didn't
drive off in the wrong way or over the cliff into the Lake.

Following the road, there was a large pine tree two and a
half miles up on Montlake where they made a left. Then
another two and a half miles, where a heavy tree hung

almost over the road. Then they made a right where a very tall redwood tree stood.

Following this road, there were no more trees until they were almost to the house, where there was an open field on both sides with fruit trees that scattered the landscape.

Once they arrived at the house, it was shrouded in a transplanted large Hawaiian banyan tree on one side and about twenty Eucalyptus trees on the roadside. This is what kept the property private.

The original owner of the land had hired a Hawaiian and Japanese landscaper because he wanted to keep it private since he thought it was sacred land.

Donnie was struck by the beauty of the place, having never ventured this far up the mountainous side of tinsel town.

The house was once used as part of a "girls camp" back in the '20s, but the city took it over and leased it out to the police department.

When they arrived, it was almost dusk, as the sun was going down over the lake and a trickle of lights was shining off in the distance.

Stepping out of the car Donnie asked, "So what about dinner?"

Jack smiled and said, "It's going to be like camping out. Tonight its frankfurters and beans. Sorry!"

Walking behind the two cops towards the cabin doors, Donnie turned towards Jack and said, "Hey it could be a lot worse!"

Music Is Life…and Death
Chapter 23

Returning to the precinct that night, Jack and Gary left the two cops behind to share the babysitting.

O'Keefe was pre-occupied when they arrived back but was anxious to learn if there were any new development.

Looking up from his desk of papers the Captain said out loud, "The word out is that Louie slipped through Wang's hands and no one knows where he is at the moment. This is not good news since Joey will probably sense the noose tightening on him unless he can resolve everything and will look to kill whoever is in his way, including Donnie. We must find Louie before anyone else is murdered."

That night in Chinatown, Wang returned and gave Chung his report and asked him what he should do with Koto's body.

Chung thought for a moment then called Joey to inform him that he had in possession, Koto and knew who killed him and that he was going to contact the cops.

Joey, who hardly ever feared anyone, began to think that he had overstepped the line this time and knew that if Chung turned over Koto that Dragna would find out and become the crime boss of Southern California.

Barcelino knew that it was time to take care of the situation once and for all.

The following morning in Brentwood, the butler answered a call from Needles California.

The caller asked if he would accept the call. A bit unusual, the stoic man's man told the caller to wait until he found Mr. Barcelino.

Fetching Joey, seemed to take forever as the morning sun was shining directly into the phone booth, where the man in the black suit wiped his forehead continuously with his handkerchief.

"Louie" came Joey's voice. "Are you Okay? What the hell happened?"

Louie replied without emotion, but with a stern voice, "It's the Chinese. I know they are following me. Any thoughts on what I should do?"

Joey thinking of a few options finally said, "Come back here first. No one knows for sure who killed Koto. Chung thinks he knows but is only guessing. Besides, the police have no clues, and it was in Nevada. We have other issues now that we need to take care of."

"Alright" replied Louie and hung up.

Joey then called Sheriff Duff to find out where the cops had taken Donnie.

Duff was not sure but had a way to find out and asked, "What else could he help him with?"

Joey replied, "I'll let you know after I hear back from you!"

By late afternoon, Duff called Joey to relay the information of where Donnie was being held.

The Sheriff had people inside the LAPD that he could call on from time to time and who were paid extra for their assistance.

Barcelino explained to Duff that for the moment he didn't need him to go there and would take care of it himself.

Duff then said, "Okay, I am standing by!"

Back at the precinct and looking through some papers on his desk, O'Keefe was sorting some things out when Jack and Gary returned mid-morning.

Jack looked at her Uncle and asked, "What is that look as if you were someplace else?"

"I was just thinking," said O'Keefe.

"The Sheriff has been a shadow in the wings ever since Koto and Bucco. Looking at the various reports, Duff appears time and time again, so I wouldn't put it past it if the Mob is paying him! I fear that he has someone inside the Department that can inform him where we have Donnie. I was not very careful in discussing this with my officers, now that I think about it and should have only enlisted a select few trustworthy guys. We probably have alerted Joey where Donnie is hiding, so I need to squelch it here by putting out a dummy order?"

O'Keefe then said, "Can you two go to the house to make sure Donnie is Ok!"

"Right," replied Jack picking up her belongings as Gary and she started running for the doors, knowing that Donnie was a sitting duck!

Music Is Life…and Death
Chapter 24

Returning to the Brentwood house, Louie had slipped through the back driveway where Joey let him in and discussed what needed to be done.

"Louie," said Joey, "After you take care of Donnie, you need to go to Chicago and let them know that everything here has been taken care of. It's very important that you do this, else we are all in trouble. Got it?"

Louie, a man a few words, replied, "Joey, why does Chicago have so much interest in this lousy songwriter? There are a dime a dozen of these meatballs out here that we could arrange a deal with?"

Joey looked Louie straight in his eyes and spoke gently and almost quietly. "Louie, the kid is related. I don't know how, I never heard it until recently, when I received a call from Florida!"

"So why rub the kid out?", asked Louie.

Joey said, "It's the principle, yet I am pretty sure that the Family would approve it once it was completed."

"But aren't you taking a big risk?" asked Louie.

"Yes and no," replied Joey. The Commission already has another songwriter and singer signed, so in a way, they would lose nothing but gain more loyalty and fewer mouths to feed if you know what I mean."

"Wow, Joey, I never thought of it that way," answered Louie.

"Okay," said Joey. "Now be on with it and call me when you get to the airport."

With that Louie went back out the same way he came while Joey waited.

Driving back up to Montlake, Jack and Gary remained in silence, alert but waiting for what they had to do next. They had already taken out their pistols. Gary's was in between his thighs, and Jack's was in her hands.

Finding the first tree in the dark, they made a hard left with the bright lights of the sedan shining as far as it could down the road. Pitch black it seemed like a half hour had gone by when they reached the second tree and began to make the right when Donnie's face came into view.

Gary slammed on the brakes, as the car's back end sled left in the turn, pushing the car sideways to a complete stop.

Jack was the first one out of the vehicle, running up to Donnie to check on him.

He was mumbling something as she wrapped her arms around him as if to say, "your safe"!

Then Gary walked up placing his gun back in his holster and said, "You alright, why are you walking out on the road? Where are the cops?"

"Hell yes, I'm okay. I was hoping to find something to eat since those damn cops left, said they'd be back and haven't returned in over two hours!"

"Christ," said Jack. "My Uncle was right!"

"Right about what?", asked Donnie

Gary replied, "That the Sheriff is in cahoots with the Mob and probably already told Joey where you were."

"So does this mean I don't get my frankfurters tonight?", Donnie asked smiling like a Cheshire cat.

They all laughed and got into the Ford and drove up to the house.

That night, after dividing up sleeping spaces, Gary who was an old cook, whipped up a campout dinner that they shared outside looking at the twinkling lights of Hollywood, along with the stars in the sky.

Following a few nightcap glasses of wine, they all turned in for the night, though the night was all but quiet and calm.

After the exquisite dinner, the three turned in, only to be awakened by a loud sound that resembled a cannon going off.

Scaring the crap out of the group, they found a very large and lost bear wondering outside the cabin looking for food. (It had escaped from the zoo, not far away).

Next came the crooked cops looking for Donnie. The plan was to kill him and collect a bonus of $20,000. After arresting them, Gary called the precinct, who then sent over the "good cops" to bring them back to the station.

Finally settling down for the rest of the night, the trio was able to get about five hours of sleep before being woken up by O'Keefe. He wanted to make sure they were okay personally.

Music Is Life…and Death
Chapter 25

Louie Lucky had been a "hitman" with the Family for
years. Barcelino only knew of him because the Miami
connection told Joey about him, so Barcelino thought that
Louie was his man, but he was very much an important
Chicago and Miami muscle man that was used by both
organizations from time to time. Hence Louie's loyalty
was to those two Families only.

Joey never knew that Louie was the eyes and ears for the
two connected Families and relayed everything back to
them – good and bad.

When Louie reported to Miami what he was to do for Joey,
he half-heartedly received permission but was assigned
another task after removing Donnie.

Naturally, he accepted and did not ask any questions or
concerns.

Back in Hollywood, around 9 AM, Captain O'Keefe was
knocking on Sheriff Duff's home door, when he walked
down the path from the free-standing garage and politely
said, "Good Morning Captain. How can I help you?"

O'Keefe trying to be funny replied, "It's the other way
around, I think. How can I help you!"

"What do you mean by that" asked Duff.

"Well to start with, your life, possibly your pension and
perhaps no jail time!", answered O'Keefe.

"What?", asked Duff with an "I didn't do anything wrong."

"Sheriff, I am placing you under arrest for cooperation with organized crime and blocking the investigation of the ongoing proceedings into Joey Barcelino and Donnie Heaven. You might also have had a hand in the death of Dick Linsky. But we can discuss all of this at the station, and hopefully, you will be the better for it when it's all said and done."

Duff knew that he could not deny most if not all of it, as the police officers took him into custody and walked him to the patrol vehicle.

Music Is Life…and Death
Chapter 26

In the morning when the Brentwood home phone rang,
Joey heard the news from one of his informant cops about
the Sheriff. He now knew he needed to act fast to take out
Donnie. He was waiting for Louie to call him from his
hotel room but was getting impatient since it was becoming
a matter of life and death.

Back in Chicago, apprehension had occurred amongst the
Commission members of the Family in the Chicago offices
of Antonio Heaven as he discussed the situation in LA.

His cousin Donnie had a contract on him for trying to be an
independent singer and for creating a company to compete
with others in the rich entertainment industry.

Like Antonio, Donnie's last name was "Cielo" meaning
sky or heavens but was changed to Heaven to be more
American. With Miami's blessing, the conversation
concluded and was agreed upon to stop the killing of
Donnie and reset the contract on Joey instead. It was
further agreed to discuss a minor arrangement with Donnie
to resolve all disputes and debt on a sliding scale that
would benefit the Family with no more than 30%, after a
period of five years.

Antonio then called Louie, who was waiting in his hotel
room at the Roosevelt. After given explicit instructions, he
hung up the phone and prepared for his next task.

When Joey didn't hear back from Louie, he sensed that
something had gone wrong and decided to call Chicago
himself. When no one would talk to him, Joey knew that
his days were numbered.

Back at the station, O'Keefe told Donnie that he could go home but would have around the clock police detail, just in case.

Donnie was nervous but accepted the new arrangement as he knew he couldn't hide out forever.

Gary and Jack weren't happy either, but after an in-depth conversation with the Captain, decided they would continue their investigation to see if there was anything else to the murders.

Deciding to visit Mr. Chung again, Jack wanted to see if he found out any more about Koto's murder.

Calling Jimmy, they arranged for another quick meeting and drove straight away that afternoon to his restaurant.

At Chung's, they found out that there was new chatter regarding the LA Family drivers and that the contract on Donnie's life had been lifted, but there was a new one in place, but no one knew who it was on.

Music Is Life…and Death
Chapter 27

Following the meeting with Chung, Gary and Jack drove back to the station to work on the case with O'Keefe.

Leaning back in a chair filing her nails, Jack was deciding what to do when a phone call came into O'Keefe's office, asking for her by name.

Picking up the phone, Jack answered, "Hello, hello?" There was no answer on the other end and then the click of the phone being hung up.

Gary saw the strange look in Jack's face asked, "Everything okay?"

"Odd, there was no one on the line," Jack replied.

"Do you want me to run it down?", asked O'Keefe

Jack just shook her head no and said, "I am thinking about going back to visit with Alice at the Canteen. Maybe she can shed just a little more on Dick's life to help us.

"Be careful Jack," Gary said as he smiled cautiously.

Driving to Cahuenga, Jack parked Big Red in the lot behind the Canteen. This time when Jack entered the old barn, she knew where to find Alice. It was late afternoon, and there were few servicemen and only a handful of women standing around and dancing. It seemed funny that it was so empty in comparison to the last time, so Jack asked Alice what had happened.

Alice almost wept as she said, "Almost 2000 of our boys left today for the Pacific. But we have been told that another 1500 or more will be here in a few days."

"The War," Jack thought. "How many more would die or be maimed before it was over? What is the real cost of any battle or war? How was her fiancé, Derek Kent? Where is he now? Did the Navy send him to a faraway land or is he still in Hawaii, safe and sound?"

Jack's mind wondered as Alice was speaking, then stopped when Alice asked?

"Are you okay?"

Jack was snapping out of her deep thoughts, replied. "Yes, just thinking of the world we live in now and how crazy it's become. Nothing really changes in history."

Jack went on, "I am sorry, but I came to ask a few more questions that perhaps could wrap up Dick's murder."

As the red Buick with the tan convertible top drove out from behind the Canteen, Jack was unaware that she was being followed.

Louie had waited outside then followed the car towards the studios on Santa Monica.

Jack didn't get any more from Alice to help in the investigation of Dick's murder, but it was a pleasant time spent with the famed actress as she drove towards 20th Century studios mindlessly.

In 1942 Spyros Skouras became president of the studio who at the time was a busy studio and the third most profitable with Cary Grant, Don Ameche, Carmen Miranda and of course Alice under contract.

Here, Jack hoped that she could obtain additional leads and perhaps reasons into the Dick Linsky murder.

Ironically, three hours before, Louie had visited the estate of Joey Barcelino, where his nephew Dr. Anthony Martino had been visiting.

While the two were out in the patio, Louie rang the doorbell. Seconds later the butler opened the door, and Louie smiled and moved his right arm from behind his back, pointed the revolver with the silencer directly at the butler and shot him dead.

Then as quietly as he could, he searched the house for Joey when he heard talking outside.

Anthony was standing with his back towards the French doors that led outside and did not see or hear Louie open them.

Joey was nonchalantly walking up the steps from the pool, when Louie pointed the gun towards Anthony, quickly pressing the trigger but moving the gun at the same time which caught Anthony in the shoulder but the impact took him to the ground as he smashed into the small table. He was out, and Louie thought dead.

Joey cursing at Louie yelled at him to stop.

Louie just smiled his evil grin and told Joey that he deserved what he was getting and as Joey rushed Louie, the gun fired off the next round and killed Joey instantly as the bullet disappeared into his face.

Louie then turned and left the house pleased with himself that the job completed except for the fate of the female private eye.

Following his instructions from Chicago, Louie drove to the nearby police station, to find out where Jack might be, then drove straight away and waited for her at the Canteen.

Back at the house, when the two maids who were cleaning the rooms upstairs in the Barcelino house heard the shots when one of them looked out into the patio and saw all the commotion by the pool.

Backing away from the windows fearing for her life, she told the older maid to be silent and waited until it was quiet, then she called the police.

After the sergeant on duty took all the information down, he rang through to O'Keefe to let him know what had happened.

The Captain immediately ran out to his car with Gary in tow, as three police cars raced to Joey's house.

After discovering the gruesome site, the police found the maids hiding and asked if they saw who did this.

The older maid said "No," but the younger one described the man who did the shooting, as she was daydreaming out the window when it took place.

Gary and O'Keefe knew then who was still around and was employed for these contract hits. Neither men knew where Jack was and became very concerned to find her before anything might happen to her.

Finding Dr. Martino injured, bloodied, but not dead, he was placed in custody for his involvement and was taken to the nearby hospital to be patched up.

Meanwhile, when Jack reached Hollywood Blvd, she decided to drive to Pico Blvd by taking Fairfax through the mansions of the rich and famous. As she eased just past the intersection of Melrose, a black Lincoln slammed into Big Red, causing the car to spin slightly. Stunned, but awake Jack's adrenaline went viral as she grabbed her purse, then opened the passenger door, crouching down sliding the revolver into her right hand and peering slightly over the door window.

She spotted the tall man approaching her car with a gun in his hand almost half smiling.

Jack prepared herself mentally for a possible battle as the man believing that she was still in the car peered through the driver's side window that was caved in with his gun pointed towards where the driver should have been.

When he didn't see her, he relaxed his hand, and his arm draped slightly downwards.

Realizing that this was the right moment, Jack stood up and looked through the passenger window and said, "Hands Up!"

When he saw Jack staring directly at him, Louie started to lift his arm, pressing his finger on the trigger to squeeze the lever.

Jack screamed at him to stop!

However not listening, Louie smiled and started to press the trigger when Jack fired one shot, hitting Louie on the right side of his head, killing him instantly.

By this time, a single police car arrived on the scene for the accident.

Jack explained to the young cops what had happened and who she was and asked him to contact Captain O'Keefe on the two-way radio.

Gary and O'Keefe were finishing up with the murders at Barcelino when the call came in.

O'Keefe asked the cop, "Is my niece alright?"

"Yes sir, but her car is banged up," the cop replied.

"Put her on," said the Captain.

When Jack took the radio, she explained everything then gave the device back to the cop.

O'Keefe instructed the cop to get Big Red towed for repairs and then the cop took Jack to the hospital.

Following these incidents, the case took a couple of days to wrap up along with the repair of the Buick.

Tired, Jack said goodbye to her Uncle, Aunt and Gary as she once again faded back to the Springs to rest.

Driving past the temperature sign next to the tram entrance to the mountain, as she entered her hometown of Palm Springs, it read 85 degrees. Jack was home.

www.ingramcontent.com/pod-product-compliance
Lightning Source LLC
Chambersburg PA
CBHW031208270326
41931CB00006B/461